I0459148

Fighting ~~with~~ for the Ones We Love

Unmasking and Defeating
Our Common Enemy

Mary Graziano Scro

Fighting for the Ones We Love:
Unmasking and Defeating Our Common Enemy

Copyright © 2023 by Mary Graziano Scro

All rights reserved.

No part of this publication may be reproduced, stored in a retrieval system, or transmitted in any form or by any means, electronic, photocopying, recording, or otherwise, without the prior permission of the copyright holder.

Unless otherwise indicated, all Scripture quotations are from the Holy Bible, New International Version (NIV) ®, Copyright © 2011, by Biblica, Inc.®. Used by permission. All rights reserved worldwide.

Scriptures referenced with (AMPC) are taken from The Amplified Bible, Old Testament, © 1965 and 1987 by The Zondervan Corporation, and from The Amplified New Testament, © 1954, 1958, 1987 by The Lockman Foundation.

Scripture verses marked (NLT) are taken from the Holy Bible, New Living Translation, copyright ©1996, 2004, 2007, 2013, 2015 by Tyndale House Foundation. All rights reserved.

Cover design by Hanna Linder Creations LLC

Author's website: www.MaryGScro.com
LinkedIn: https://www.linkedin.com/in/mary-scro-0916
Facebook: https://www.facebook.com/mary.scro.12

To all those who poured Jesus' love and truth into me.
I am passing it on.
And to my readers…may you go and do likewise.

Contents

The Unseen Battle

How can we keep from fighting with and hurting people we love most, over and over again? How do we gain and maintain peace in all our relationships?

Good questions! I imagine you've asked them, too. While I definitely don't have all the answers, I had a revelation about the true source of most of the conflict in our relationships: Satan, the devil, the enemy of our souls. His mission is to steal, kill and destroy relationships, and he does this through lying to us and preying on our weaknesses. Our assignment, should we choose to accept it, is to stop the devil through learning to recognize how he manipulates us and defeat him in God's strength. We need to learn to unmask and fight the *true* enemy, not the people we love.

This book is not intended to be an all-inclusive book about spiritual warfare in general, but to focus on the warfare specifically related to our relationships with God and each other. Satan will attack our closest relationships every single day—he prowls around like a roaring lion looking for someone to devour (1 Peter 5:8). My goal for these pages is to increase your awareness of this daily warfare and help equip you to make better choices *when* the battles come. We often aid and abet Satan's attack on our relationships when we fall for his lies and fight *with* our loved ones instead of *for* them, on their side.

When our relationships are strong and secure—first and foremost, our relationship with God—we can better show the world what God's love looks like. And I think we can all agree that the world desperately needs to know God's love!

Why is awareness and equipping important? Just as a parent on an airplane must first put on their own oxygen mask before they can help their child, you must first be able to walk in the love and authority God gave you so you can better love others. In other words, if you had to choose between two people to help *you* on your journey toward better relationships—one who exuded confidence in God and enjoyed other people, or one who didn't get along with people at all and talked down about them—which would you choose?

God showed me that becoming a confident-in-God person who loves with His love doesn't happen overnight. Spiritual maturity comes when we're intentional about continuing to grow closer to Him every day through Bible study, faith, and choosing to obey what He tells us to do. No matter when we start our journey with Jesus, it's important that we keep growing. The stronger our faith, the more readily we can resist the enemy and love others like God loves us. We can see more clearly how the cultural definitions of love and tolerance conflict with God's definitions, and help people discover God's truth. We can stop fighting with people and instead unmask and fight the real enemy who is influencing them. We'll be ready to disciple others in truth and help them draw closer to God as well.

Some of my testimonies describe how I "hear" God's voice. He speaks to me in many ways—through His Word, through people, through dreams, and as a still, small voice in my thoughts. How do I know it's God? By faith, in hindsight, and through experience as I've obeyed (or not) what I've heard Him say. I've learned to always let Scripture be my final authority; may it be yours as well.

Where possible I tried not to use the term "Christian" because it is overused and watered down in our culture. Jesus called His followers disciples, and charged them to go make disciples. So where you see "Christian", I am referring to a disciple of Jesus whose life reflects their growing relationship with Him.

I'll end each chapter with a suggested prayer you can say to invite Jesus into your journey. Feel free to add your own words from your heart as you reflect on what He shows you.

May the Lord bless you as you read and give you greater revelation of His ways. May you learn to stand strong and win the daily spiritual battles so you can enjoy peace in all your relationships!

Dear Jesus,

I long for deeper relationships, filled with peace and joy instead of strife and anger. Please teach me how to walk in Your ways and how to recognize Your voice above all others. And help me to be aware of when the enemy is seeking to use me to steal, kill, and destroy those You've brought into my life. Open my heart to what you want to show me through this book, and through your Word.

In Your name I pray, Amen.

1

Why Do We Fight?

"Ready, aim, FIRE!"

Sounds of gunfire ring throughout the battlefield, along with yells and shouts as the good guys on horseback charge the enemy forces to drive them back. Just as determined, those defending the fort quickly reload and prepare to fire another round on the attacking forces. Soldiers on opposing sides valiantly charge toward one another, ready to die for their causes.

Step forward a few centuries into the world of movies and fly out into the galaxy. One-man enemy fighters dart back and forth, shooting lasers at the Starship Enterprise. Shields are up but weakening. The ship's insides shake, jolting the crew with each blow. Captain Kirk vows he will not surrender.

Step into another world, through scenes from *The Lord of the Rings* movies, as orcs are on the rampage to destroy everything good at the command of the evil Sauron. The dwarfs, elves, hobbits, and humans join forces to defend their freedom.

Wow, there's nothing like an action-packed battle scene to keep you on the edge of your seat!

When I first became a disciple of Jesus, I viewed spiritual warfare as an offensive battle, much like what I saw in the movies. Thoughts of battle against our enemy, the devil, were energizing and exciting. I was in the "Army of God," and the enemy was going *down*. I looked up and devoured any Bible verses that talked about demons fleeing, deliverance, and setting the captives free. I sought out people who could mentor me, godly warriors with testimonies about their experiences defeating demons. Yes, I was well on my way to becoming Super Mary, the Demon Slayer.

Years later, I agreed to co-teach a women's physical/spiritual fitness class at our church. When the Lord impressed upon me to teach about spiritual warfare, I just *knew* it was because I had so much experience and so much to teach. I even had a title: "Prepare for Battle!" I had an outline of topics, including "What is Spiritual Warfare?" and "We are in a Battle, We DO Have an Enemy!" I conducted a small survey at the beginning of the first class to help me determine the level of everyone's understanding and find out what they wanted to know. Then all I needed to do was fill in the details, and I was ready to *impart* from my vast store of knowledge.

But I had completely missed the point: The purpose of engaging in spiritual battle is not just to win. The purpose of spiritual warfare is to win *souls* into the Kingdom of God!

And we do that through love, and love requires relationships. In Jesus' words:

One of the teachers of the law came and heard them debating. Noticing that Jesus had given them a good answer, he asked him, "Of all the commandments, which is the most important?"

"The most important one," answered Jesus, "is this: 'Hear, O Israel: The Lord our God, the Lord is one. Love the Lord your God with all your heart and with all your soul and with all your mind and with all your strength.' The second is this: 'Love your neighbor as yourself.' There is no commandment greater than these."
—Mark 12:28-31

God disarmed my battle plan and showed me a totally different plan that centers on His love for me and my intimacy with Him. Only then can I love and fight for others, in His strength and with His wisdom. In typical God fashion, He revealed His plan to me one week at a time. And, knowing I like acronyms, He arranged the topic titles to spell warfare.

- Wearing Your Armor and Wielding Your Weapons. Know who you are, and what He's given you.
- Awareness of the Real Enemy. And it's not people.
- Resting in the Lord. The battle has already been won.
- Facing Your Enemy, Not Fearing Him. God is bigger.

- <u>A</u>udible—the Power of the Spoken Word. Bring life, not death, with your words.
- <u>R</u>ejoicing in the Lord Always. Be thankful that your name is written in the Book of Life.
- <u>E</u>ntertainment, or <u>E</u>xposure to Temptation. Be aware of the impact of what you read, watch, and listen to—what values and lifestyles you "take in."

God's Way to Fight

God's way of winning battles is not like ours. Unlike these movie scenes where the good guys win through destroying the enemy forces, our Hero won victory through His own death in the most epic battle scene in the history of the world: the Crucifixion.

But if Jesus won the war, isn't the enemy already defeated?

Yes, Jesus gave us a once-and-for-all victory with the Crucifixion and Resurrection, and we can walk daily in that victory and in Jesus' authority. But, for now, our enemy still has power as the "prince of this world." We can't underestimate the devil's passion to destroy unbelievers whom God loves—often using Jesus' disciples to help him—and his ability to render believers ineffective in loving others.

God's goal, through us, is to bring His Kingdom to earth and love people into that Kingdom. Our enemy's (the devil's) goal is to stop the Kingdom of God from advancing and completely destroy what God values most: loving relationships.

The most powerful force in the universe is God's love—God *is* love (1 John 4:8). His love and power are activated when we choose to walk in 1 Corinthians 13:4-8—love, the selfless love that sent Jesus to the cross:

> Love is patient, love is kind.
>
> It does not envy, it does not boast, it is not proud.
>
> It does not dishonor others, it is not self-seeking, it is not easily angered, it keeps no record of wrongs. Love does not delight in evil but rejoices with the truth.
>
> It always protects, always trusts, always hopes, always perseveres.
>
> Love never fails.

The devil and his army relentlessly attack this love at all levels in our everyday lives, including attacking God's love for us and our ability to receive that love. If we aren't aware of Satan's tactics, we can aid and abet him in his mission to steal, kill, and destroy us and our relationships. The Lord called us to advance His Kingdom here on the earth and to make Him known to those who desperately need Him. We can't do that if we are uninformed, and if, in our ignorance, we hurt those we are called to love. We also can't give what we haven't received and fully accepted—if we aren't filled with God's love and secure in our relationship with Him, it's impossible for us to love others with His love.

Be Prepared for Battle

Jesus wants us to live each day fully prepared to recognize and stand firm against whatever comes our way from a vicious enemy who hates God and hates us. Jesus is our Commander-in-Chief, and He provides everything we need to be victorious when we humbly submit to God, walk in humility with others, and resist the enemy.

> All of you, clothe yourselves with humility toward one another, because,
> "God opposes the proud but shows favor to the humble."
> Humble yourselves, therefore, under God's mighty hand, that he may lift you up in due time. Cast all your anxiety on him because he cares for you. Be alert and of sober mind. Your enemy the devil prowls around like a roaring lion looking for someone to devour. Resist him, standing firm in the faith….
> —1 Peter 5:5-9

Keeping in mind God's goal (to teach us unconditional love), and the enemy's goal (to destroy love), let's learn more about how to recognize and stand down that roaring lion and rescue people from his grasp.

The remaining chapters of this book follow the outline of W.A.R.F.A.R.E. topics, and include biblical references, practical steps, and personal testimony. Chapters don't need to be read in order, feel free to browse as the Lord leads.

Let the journey begin!

Dear Jesus,

I am ready to learn new ways—Your ways—for loving others. Teach me how to grow in Your love. Show me how to recognize, face, and stand down the enemy when he comes to steal, kill, and destroy the people You love through my sinful words and actions. I want to learn how to have better relationships through Your strength and not my own.

In Your name I pray, Amen.

2

Wearing Your Armor and Wielding Your Weapons (WARFARE)

I don't know about you, but I would never consider leaving my house naked. Without clothes on, I'd be vulnerable and exposed for all to see.

In the same way, I'm vulnerable if I'm not wearing my spiritual armor. So why don't I put it on every day before I leave the house? Why don't I make time daily to read the Bible and pray? When I don't, I am exposed to an enemy that delights in causing me and those around me misery and pain. If we don't take care of ourselves, learn how to submit to God, and learn how to stand down the lion who comes against us, we cannot help or teach anyone else.

In one of the most well-known passages of Scripture, Paul advises us on how to arm and protect ourselves. He starts with the "who, what, and why" of our battles.

Finally, be strong in the Lord and in his mighty power. Put on the full armor of God, so that you can take your stand against the devil's schemes. For our struggle is not against flesh and blood, but against the rulers, against the authorities, against the powers of this dark world and against the spiritual forces of evil in the heavenly realms.

—Ephesians 6:10-12

- Who has the power? The Lord, not me.
- What do we need to access His power? The full armor of God, by faith.
- Why do we need armor? So we can take a stand against our true enemy, the devil, and the evil spiritual powers in the heavenly realms (not people).

Without these first verses, the armor Paul tells us to put on and the weapons he tells us to wield are useless and will not be effective in battle. Paul continues to describe the armor:

Therefore put on the full armor of God, so that when the day of evil comes, you may be able to stand your ground, and after you have done everything, to stand. Stand firm then, with the belt of truth buckled around your waist, with the breastplate of righteousness in place, and with your feet fitted with the readiness that comes from the gospel of peace. In addition to all this, take up the shield of faith, with which you can extinguish all the flaming arrows of the evil one. Take the helmet of salvation and the sword of the Spirit, which is the word of God.

And pray in the Spirit on all occasions with all kinds of prayers and requests. With this in mind, be alert and always keep on praying for all the Lord's people.

—Ephesians 6:13-18

Each piece of armor has a purpose, and is vital to enabling us to defend ourselves, defeat our enemy, and love those whom God sends our way. Here's a brief description of each piece and how it helps and protects us.

…with the **_belt of truth_** buckled around your waist…

This belt holds the breastplate and other armor in place. We must know the truth about the Lord and about who we are in Him. That truth must be firmly secured in our minds and in our hearts. When it is, we can walk with great confidence…and love. Without it, the other pieces of armor can fall off (be ineffective), leaving us unprotected and vulnerable.

…with the **_breastplate of righteousness_** in place…

This breastplate covers the heart, the seat of our will and the source of our life/blood. We are righteous because we received *His* righteousness when we were saved. We walk in right relationship with Him, knowing He is the source of our life and the protector of our hearts. When loving others causes us heartache, the breastplate protects our hearts—we know we are still His and can walk in His peace, no matter what happens.

…and with your ***feet fitted*** with the readiness that comes from the ***gospel of peace***… ("shoes" of the gospel of peace)

Feet fitted with the gospel of peace give us the ground where we tread and bring the Lord with us into every situation as we actively walk forward. The Gospel is the truth of His love and salvation; and when we walk forward to proclaim that truth, we bring His peace and walk in His love.

…take up the ***shield of faith,*** with which you can extinguish all the flaming arrows of the evil one…

This shield protects us from the arrows of lies, hurt, and pain the enemy shoots at us every day, often wielded by those closest to us. When we choose to say "No, God says…" our shield of faith is raised to defend us against these arrows. We can press forward toward others without fear.

…Take the ***helmet of salvation***…

This helmet represents what Christ did for us on the Cross. It protects our head, which houses our mind and thinking. Once we have been saved, we have the mind of Christ, and therefore have the ability to know, think, and believe the truth. The head is also the most vulnerable to fatal injury. With salvation, we cannot be eternally lost (fatally wounded)—we are assured of Heaven. Thus, we can walk boldly forward with no fear of what the enemy can do. We are eternally safe.

…and the ***sword of the Spirit***, which is the word of God…

This sword is the Bible, and it is one of two weapons Paul mentions. The Bible is God's love story to us. First and foremost, we read His Word to know Him and to know Jesus and to know who we are as God's children and heirs. I believe to "take" the sword of the spirit means to have His Word in my heart—read it, know it, meditate on the truths it contains. We buy the enemy's lies because we haven't read the Bible enough to know the truth about God and about ourselves. The more we study the Bible with that purpose—knowing God—the more we'll be able to bring the truth to others in a loving way. Then this powerful weapon can be used as God intended.

If we don't read the Bible with the purpose of knowing God, His truth becomes a weapon in our hands for the enemy to direct. The enemy knows God and knows the Bible and is ready at every turn to twist it for his destructive purposes. It's easy to go out swinging blindly and wildly, using Bible verses out of context or for the wrong reasons, including to support our own or others' opinions or sinful behavior. When we do, the very ones we are trying to help are likely to get hurt. Being a bold extrovert, I know this from experience, as you'll see throughout this book.

…And ***pray in the Spirit*** on all occasions with all kinds of prayers and requests. With this in mind, be alert and always ***keep on praying*** for all the saints….

Our ultimate weapon is prayer because prayer connects us with God. When we pray in the Spirit for others and for ourselves, we acknowledge our dependence on God and exercise the authority Jesus gave us. Ongoing prayer from a heart connected to God activates His power in our lives and helps us remember Who is ultimately in control. Pray throughout the day, for everyone, about anything and everything, in the Spirit. (God leads, we pray as He leads.) Not sure how to pray in the Spirit? Ask the Holy Spirit to teach you and guide you, and believe He will.

Choosing to Wear the Armor

Overall, the armor of God is activated by faith. While we are told to "put on" the armor, it's really about choosing every day to believe in what we already have. The weapons are ours to use as He leads. As we grow in understanding of the Word of God and prayer—by reading the Bible, believing what it says, and obeying what Jesus teaches—our faith to trust God and believe in the strength of our armor will grow. Jesus gives us this encouragement:

> "If you love me, keep my commands. And I will ask the Father, and he will give you another advocate to help you and be with you forever— the Spirit of truth. The world cannot accept him, because it neither sees him nor knows him. But you know him, for he lives with you and will be in you. I will not leave you as orphans; I will come to you. Before long, the world will not see me anymore, but you will see me. Because I live, you also will live. On that day you will realize that I am in my Father, and you are in me, and

I am in you. Whoever has my commands and keeps them is the one who loves me. The one who loves me will be loved by my Father, and I too will love them and show myself to them."
—John 14:15-21

I have yet to fully understand these verses, although I've read them many times. I receive what it says about my relationship with God and with Jesus by faith and trust that I have the armor—righteousness, salvation, shield, shoes, truth—and the weapons to walk in victory. I also do my best to obey God's commands to show Him how much I love Him.

When we don't believe, demonstrated by not donning our armor by faith, we find ourselves tangled up in self-condemnation, pride, lies, and judgment of others instead of throwing ourselves fully on God's grace and mercy. Without faith, we know we do wrong, but forget that the wrong was paid for *in full* by Jesus. Without it, we allow the enemy's lies to strip away the freedom that Christ died to give us. Without it, we are defeated before we *start*.

Why Do We Still Get Attacked?

If we know all this and understand the armor, why do we still get beat up? Here are just four possible reasons:

- We're human, therefore we forget, and we don't practice every day. Maybe we don't fully believe in who we are in Christ. Or it could just be we're lazy. All of the above for me. Add to that, we have a deceptive enemy who waits for any opportunity to throw lies and condemnation at us, especially about our identity in Christ. Unlike our gracious God, Satan is extremely law-bound and legalistic. He knows what sin is, and at every turn he waits to throw the sin or mistake in our faces. For example, "You really hurt her feelings, you're a horrible friend" or, "That's gossip—and you call yourself a disciple of Jesus?" or, "You forgot your mother's birthday—only an awful daughter would do that." His goal is to condemn us, not only for our behavior, but for who we *are*. While the Holy Spirit convicts us gently of our sin (what we did), with the goal of restoring our relationship with God, the enemy of our souls condemns us (who we are) with the hopes that we'll stay defeated instead of repenting and turning to God.

- We just had a *mountaintop* experience, a time when we know we've experienced the presence of the Lord. Whether after a powerful time of worship, a life-changing conference, or a successful event in our lives, we can easily let our guard down after that moment and become vulnerable to Satan's attacks.

- Our pride is up—we rely way too much on ourselves to sustain what God never intends to be a daily practice. Sometimes we try to duplicate what God did through us or continue in a direction where He's not leading us. When we step out in our own strength, our pride makes us an easy target for the devil's condemnation and deception.

- Sometimes we just go on vacation, either physically or mentally, and act out-of-line with who we are in Christ. Again, we let our guard down. We can also forget that it's not about *our* strength; it's about divine power.

For though we live in the world, we do not wage war as the world does. The weapons we fight with are not the weapons of the world. On the contrary, they have divine power to demolish strongholds.

—2 Corinthians 10:3-4

And His grace (divine power to live as He says) is more evident when we are weak, as Paul discovered.

Even if I should choose to boast, I would not be a fool, because I would be speaking the truth. But I refrain, so no one will think more of me than is warranted by what I do or say, or because of these surpassingly great revelations. Therefore, in order to keep me from becoming conceited, I was given a thorn in my flesh, a messenger of Satan, to torment me. Three times I pleaded with the Lord to take it away from me. But he said to me, "My grace is sufficient for you, for my power is made perfect in weakness." Therefore I will boast all the more gladly about my weaknesses, so that Christ's power may rest on me. That is why, for Christ's sake, I delight in weaknesses,

in insults, in hardships, in persecutions, in diffi-
culties. For when I am weak, then I am strong.
                              —2 Corinthians 12:6-10

Knowing Your Weaknesses

When we are without our armor, the enemy can and
will beat us up, lie to us, and render us ineffective to do
anything God calls us to do. That's why it's important
to not only wear our armor, but to know when we are
most vulnerable. For me, that time is in the mornings
when I first open my eyes...before I've had time to even
think about getting dressed spiritually.

Years ago, I had an affectionate and demonstrative
cat named Little Bit. As soon as I moved ever so slightly
or opened my eyes in the mornings, she started her
walk up the bed toward my face, meowing the entire
way to make it clear she knew I was awake. Whether I
was truly awake or just stirring didn't matter to her—
she saw signs of life and reacted to them immediately.

In some ways, our enemy is no different than Little
Bit. If I did something wrong the day before or spoke
harsh words, or didn't quite "get it right" in whatever I
did, the enemy starts bombarding my mind with accusations and condemnation about yesterday (which I
can't change) while I'm still half asleep. If I mull over
those thoughts instead of praying, believing, and taking
up my sword of truth, then my own sinful nature and
pride take over. I miss out on what the Lord may be
speaking and waste valuable time and energy. And if
I'm not careful, the self-condemnation affects my whole
day. I've regrettably wounded co-workers and friends

through the years because I allowed the enemy to set the tone for my day.

I am also vulnerable when I focus more on knowing Bible facts instead of knowing the Author of the Book. Knowing truth just to know truth puffs up our pride; knowing the Author of Scripture humbles us. I've used God's Word out of context and without love, wounding others and myself, during seasons of truth-seeking. In 1 Corinthians 13, Paul compares speaking without love to a noisy gong or clanging cymbal. Yes, that's me, far more often than I'd like to admit.

I am also quick to forget my armor when I feel threatened or insecure. I can lash out at those closest to me, or try to control my circumstances and others, or refuse to listen. In my sin, I've spoken words I wish I could take back and left wounded people in my wake.

Thankfully, over the years the Lord has healed my heart and changed me from the inside out as I've pursued Him, stayed in His Word, prayed, surrounded myself with others who know Him, and obeyed the best I could. My words are changing and I am becoming more loving. As a result, I'm seeing less and less of the old me and enjoying increasing times of victory over past sin. The process has been a glorious, hard, amazing, and transforming journey. And the fruit is more joy in my heart and peace in my relationships.

But I still mess up. (And you will too; we all do.)

As soon as I do, the enemy is right there with his accusations: "See, you haven't changed. You're so full of yourself, and God opposes the proud. You'll never change—He can't use you!" Does this sound familiar? I've heard these seemingly internal accusations so many times you'd think I'd recognize the condemnation right away by now. Unfortunately, sometimes in my self-pity I entertain the idea that I'm useless for quite a while before I realize I've been listening to the wrong voice. But once I recognize it, I whip out that Sword of the Spirit and I declare the Lord's truth about myself: I'm His child, His beloved, and I am forgiven. I pray to Him—I thank Him for Who He is and all He does, I confess my sins, and I ask for His forgiveness. I go to those I've wounded and ask for their forgiveness. I ask God to continue His healing work in me. I stand down that lion before he can get anywhere close enough to devour me.

And then I let it go. Sometimes letting go takes a few minutes, and sometimes it takes a whole lot longer. The point is to keep believing, keep declaring, keep praying until you are able to let go.

The enemy remembers every wrong thing we've ever done, and He knows how to push our buttons to get us to condemn ourselves or others. His goal is to keep us looking back, keep us beating ourselves up for what we can't change. The more we look back, the more paralyzed we become...unable to move forward into what God has planned for us.

Each piece of armor is a reminder of who we are in Christ and Whose we are as a child of the King. The weapons of the Word and prayer activate His power in our lives—a power greater than we are, greater than anything we face. Without the armor and weapons, the enemy can devour us: steal our joy and peace, and destroy our relationships. With this protection, we are invincible.

Don't you feel like praying to Him now as a reminder of who you are in Him?

Dear Jesus,

Help me turn to You first every morning, and train me to seek You all day as needed. Teach me more about the armor You gave me, and show me how to wear it confidently. Show me where and when I'm most vulnerable, and where I have blind spots. Thank You for the armor, and for Your Word, and for the privilege of being Your child and the open invitation to come to You in prayer. May I know You more every day!

In Your name I pray, Amen.

3

Awareness of
the Real Enemy
(wArfare)

Be well balanced (temperate, sober of mind), be
vigilant and cautious at all times; for that enemy
of yours, the devil, roams around like a lion
roaring [in fierce hunger], seeking someone to
seize upon and devour.
> —1 Peter 5:8 AMPC

Satan, the enemy of our souls, is seeking to devour
us. At all times. He shows no mercy and has many
battle tactics, some of which are designed to get us to aid
and abet him in his mission to hurt others. One way the
enemy brings destruction is to begin his lies with truth.

Yes, you read that correctly. While the enemy ultimately lies, sometimes he uses truth to get our attention and to bait us into falling for his lies—lies about
ourselves and others. He concocts a unique blend of lies
and truth that can quickly defeat us if we are not aware
of this tactic.

Here is an example of lies mixed with truth. At times, my words can be abrupt and harsh. Sometimes it's because I have my mind on something else, or I've been interrupted, or maybe I'm just tired. Whatever the reason, I've sinned and the enemy knows that. So, at the first opportunity, the internal running commentary starts:

> *What you said to LeAnne yesterday was really mean. (Fact — I sinned)*

> *You know, you are always saying mean things. (Any time you hear always in your head, or verbally, there's a good chance it's a lie. But since you already feel badly, you buy it. And it doesn't stop here.)*

> *You're just a mean person.*

With that last lie, the enemy has moved from attacking what I did to attacking who I am. If I'm not careful, my mind will spin around and around in purposeless self-condemnation.

The Lord taught me how to defend myself: agree with what is true and bring good out of it. So, I'll respond to the enemy by saying aloud: "Thank you for pointing out my bad behavior. I'm going to confess that sin now, pray for LeAnne, and apologize to her."

"Oh, and by the way, Jesus loves me and I am precious in His sight. I declare that I am not a mean person, but a loveable child of the King."

I've found the more I do this, the less the enemy uses this tactic. The last thing he wants is for us to humbly confess our sins, pray for others, and humbly reach out to them for forgiveness.

Another one of Satan's tactics is to bait us into being offended. I've started my own running commentaries far too often when I've felt snubbed by a friend or snapped at by my husband, Don. I've not been aware of who initiated these thoughts, I just went with them.

> *I can't believe she just did that—walked right by me without even saying hello! I thought we were good friends. Wonder what I've done? Oh, I know, it must have been when _____. Okay, if that's how she wants to be, FINE! I don't need her anyway.*
>
> *And God, why didn't You do something? Don't You care that she's treating me like this?*
>
> *God, did You hear how Don just talked to me? That's it! I'm not speaking to him right now.*

Recognizing the Battle

Whether or not we see, feel, or even acknowledge the spiritual battle when misunderstandings happen between us and others, the source of the conflict is often spiritual. We are quick to take offense when something doesn't go our way, or we get prideful and think a situation is all about us. Then we get angry or put up walls, and we blame God and others. The enemy attacks through strangers, enemies, and even our closest friends and family members to hit us at our weakest moments.

Then he uses us like pawns in a chess game to exact revenge.

Armed with this awareness, let's go back and re-write the earlier running commentaries.

I can't believe she walked right by me without even saying hello! I thought we were good friends. Wait— we ARE good friends. She must have a lot on her mind—not speaking to me is so unlike her. I wonder how I can help. God, show me what to do. Please help her with whatever she is going through right now.

Wow, Don must really be having a rough day to speak to me like that. God, help me to love him and show me how to pray for him.

Our enemy also pits us against each other in a much more subtle way, through unseen battles in the spiritual realm. God revealed the battle to me one day on my walk in a neighborhood park.

As I walked along the path, my friend Su came to mind. Nothing specific, but I started to feel angry at her with no reason. Then thoughts about how she did this or that, said this or that, and *how dare she?* invaded my peaceful ponderings and took over.

I heard someone approaching from behind during this thought process, then he passed me and kept going. When he was out of sight, I stopped and shook my head. The negative thoughts about Su were gone. I didn't even remember what I had been thinking! Stunned, I asked the Lord what just happened. He whispered to my mind, *The man who ran past you was very angry. When he got in your space, his demons of anger attacked your mind.* In my spirit, I knew this was true. I had no reason to be angry at Su, and the thoughts were only in my mind as that man ran by.

God also revealed this type of unseen battle on other occasions as I've prayed about why some people seem to cause a reaction in me, but only when I'm around them. Two examples from my life come to mind.

Years ago, I'd travel home to visit my parents about four times a year. During those trips home, loving and positive thoughts about them brought a smile to my face. I couldn't wait to see them! But as soon as I walked in the door I became angry. Frustrated, I kept asking God to "fix me." When I was ready to receive the truth, He showed me I held unforgiveness in my heart toward them that blocked my ability to love them. Over time, He brought healing to my heart as I chose to forgive my parents…mostly for things they didn't even know they did. Now my thoughts, both when I'm away from them and with them, reflect my love for them.

I can also feel impatient or frustrated with people whom I think differently about when I'm not with them. I've talked to others who have experienced this. For example, I know someone who struggles with a sense of self-worth. I pray for him and know he's a tender-hearted and loving person inside. And then, when I'm around him and he acts out of his insecurity, I some-times get negative thoughts out of the blue, tempting me to agree with and feed his insecurity. If I'm not aware of the origin of those thoughts and don't nip them in the bud by choosing to think the truth about who he is, I can easily allow the enemy to use me to hurt my friend. I don't even have to speak the negative thoughts; my facial expressions and impatience will telegraph my thoughts without me saying a word.

Now, I don't want you to panic that demons are everywhere and can influence and attack at any time. I want you to be *aware* that demons are everywhere and can influence and attack at any time. *But, they can only succeed if you are unaware and thereby let them.* Know that God's angels are also everywhere, ready to minister to you when you need help (Hebrews 1:13).

Knowing Satan's Strategy

We all need to grow in awareness that our common enemy, the devil, is the real culprit. We must remember his goal is to destroy relationships. Let's step back for a moment and look again at Ephesians 6:12:

> *For our struggle is not against flesh and blood,* but against the rulers, against the authorities, against the powers of this dark world and against the spiritual forces of evil in the heavenly realms (*emphasis added*).

When I would read this verse, I used to skip past the first nine words to get to the warfare part. But without those first nine words, we miss the whole point of what Paul is communicating. Let's step a little further back in Ephesians.

In Ephesians 5 and the first part of Ephesians 6, Paul writes about relationships and walking in love. In general, he instructs us to "live a life of love, just as

Christ loved us" (verse 2), "speak to one another with psalms, hymns, and spiritual songs" (verse 19), and to "submit to one another out of reverence for Christ" (verse 21). Then Paul provides specific instruction about husbands and wives, fathers and children, slaves and masters. The overall theme is how to walk with each other in healthy and God-pleasing relationships.

Now let's step back even further, all the way back to the beginning in Genesis. After God's work of creation, "Adam and his wife were both naked, and they felt no shame" (Genesis 2:25). Then after the serpent's deception, Adam responded to God's call by saying, "I heard you in the garden, and I was afraid because I was naked; so I hid" (Genesis 3:10). Then, Adam blames God and Eve for his own sin of eating the forbidden fruit: "The woman you put here with me—she gave me some fruit from the tree, and I ate it" (Genesis 2:12).

What was the purpose of the first attack on Adam and Eve? To destroy relationships—between God and them first, then between Adam and Eve.

Our enemy's strategy hasn't changed since his attack in the garden. Paul knew of the enemy's goal to destroy relationships any way he can. It's with that awareness that he intentionally started Ephesians 6:12 with a caution that we are not to be fighting against people. In continuing with the armor of God picture that marvelously describes our relationship with God through Jesus, Paul also reminds us that our battles are not against God. God is our protector, our salvation, our truth, and our righteousness. He is never our enemy.

Satan, our enemy, is out to stop us from loving God and loving others because he knows love never fails (1

Corinthians 13:8), love is the greatest gift (1 Corinthians 13:13), and love has the power to cover a multitude of sins (1 Peter 4:8).

When we focus on God's love and on obeying His commandments to love Him and others, we can more easily recognize and respond to the Holy Spirit's leading. His way is always to love, to forgive, to overlook the offense, to turn the other cheek, and to walk in peace. Relationships are restored instead of destroyed, and preserved instead of broken. Many times, the person who hurt us isn't aware of it; and often, we aren't aware when we've hurt others.

Sadly, in some relationships, no matter what you or I do, the other person refuses to listen. But this does not negate our responsibility to love and pray for those whom God places in our path, until *He* says to stop. There are times to persevere and times to walk away (and shake the dust off your feet). Unless we're aware of the enemy's tactics, we'll miss God's heart and intentions for others.

You are only responsible for your own actions, not for anyone else's. Resolve to walk in love, aware that you have an enemy and it's not people or God. Be secure in God's provision to defeat the real enemy through you when you keep His two greatest commandments and do things His way. Then we can, indeed, accomplish *God's* goal in our daily battles: to bring His Kingdom to earth and love people into it.

Dear Jesus,

Thank You for always speaking the truth to me when I come to You. Help me to recognize the lies quickly as I hear them, and before I act on them. Help me to know You and Your Word so well that I can boldly stand against the lies and grow in awareness of where the battlefront is in my life. Help me to be quick to repent and quick to forgive no matter what others may do.

In Your name I pray, Amen.

4

Resting in the Lord
(WA**R**FARE)

Recently, Don and I watched a football game. Not just any game, but a Southeast Conference (SEC) rivalry game between Auburn and Georgia. We were perched on the edge of our seats, rooting for Georgia. With less than a minute left in the game, Auburn, down by one point, was about to make its final effort with a fourth down and 18 yards to go. We stood up, prepared to high-five a Georgia victory.

The pass is up, it's intercep...wait, no, the ball is tipped, the receiver has it, and it's an Auburn...touch-down? In just a few short seconds, the lead changed and our team was losing. The announcers had no words for what we'd all just witnessed. Stunned, we slumped back into our seats.

But wait, there were still 25 seconds left on the clock for a Georgia comeback. Back to the edge of our seats, we watched as they moved quickly down the field into scoring position. With three seconds left, the ball was snapped, the quarterback scrambled, and, and...(sigh).

Down he went as he passed the ball a few yards ahead into the turf.

Game over. Auburn won, Georgia lost. What an emotional roller coaster.

In contrast, watching that game reminded me of watching the Masters one year. But instead of watching "live," I video-taped the end of the match so I already knew who won. From that position, I peacefully sat back and enjoyed the golfer's victory. No emotional ups and downs, no surprises. In one sense, knowing the outcome robbed me of some of the excitement. But already knowing who won allowed me to watch the match from a totally different perspective: one of confidence that no matter where each of the winner's shots ended up, ultimately the shots would be good enough for a victory.

Maybe you're not a sports fan. Have you ever read a book and skipped to the end to see what happened, then gone back and read through? Maybe you've watched a movie for a second time (or third, or fourth). With a book or movie, you read or watch with less nervous anticipation when you already know the ending.

That's the perspective the Lord wants us to have about spiritual warfare: complete and total confidence in Jesus' victory on the Cross, even when we can't see where the next shot is going or coming from. The Lord wants us to be so filled with His love for us that we have an overflow to pour out to others. That perspective grows the more we learn how to enter into His rest. True biblical rest is formed in us when we do the following:

- Receive God's love through a relationship with Jesus.
- Expect God's provision.
- Stay content where we are and set out only at His direction.
- Trust Him fully with everything.

Receiving the Relationship

First and foremost, rest is the act of fully and deliberately receiving the relationship Jesus made possible for us through His death and resurrection. When we do this, we are seated with Christ in the heavenly realms (Ephesians 2:6). We do not *earn* our right to be there, we simply receive salvation that immediately places us in right relationship with God. In Ephesians 2, Paul reminds us once again that it is God's grace that saves us—it is His gift to us:

> As for you, you were dead in your transgressions and sins, in which you used to live when you followed the ways of this world and of the ruler of the kingdom of the air, the spirit who is now at work in those who are disobedient. All of us also lived among them at one time, gratifying the cravings of our flesh and following its desires and thoughts. Like the rest, we were by nature deserving of wrath. But because of his great love for us, God, who is rich in mercy, made us alive with Christ even when we were dead in transgressions—it is by grace you have been saved. And God raised us up with Christ and seated us

with him in the heavenly realms in Christ Jesus, in order that in the coming ages he might show the incomparable riches of his grace, expressed in his kindness to us in Christ Jesus. For it is by grace you have been saved, through faith—and this is not from yourselves, it is the gift of God—not by works, so that no one can boast. For we are God's handiwork, created in Christ Jesus to do good works, which God prepared in advance for us to do.

—Ephesians 2:1-10

When someone gives you a gift, do you try to pay them for it? Of course not! Then why do we try to pay God for our salvation by trying to earn it? We need to believe that by the power of His grace alone, we can securely rest in our relationship with God through Jesus. We don't have to earn our rest, or perform for God to earn our position as His child. We simply receive.

Performing for acceptance has been a struggle for me for as long as I can remember. I've heard amazing stories from people who received salvation and immediately understood God's grace. They glowed with His love, His forgiveness, and His mercy. But oh, not me. I was determined to be the best Jesus follower on the planet. Even though I was saved, I still felt a need to prove I was good enough.

One day, several years ago, as I sat and watched TV, the Lord spoke to me in His still small voice.

You have an idol in your life.

I knew it—I'm watching way too much TV. That's it, Lord, isn't it? You told me to cut back, and I didn't listen. You said TV was a problem for me, and here I am still watching it. I can't believe I messed this up. Again!

As I paced around my apartment (after turning off the TV, of course), feeling condemned and lamenting my failure, He spoke again.

Your idol is Mary the Perfect Christian.

WHAT???

Stunned into silence, I stopped mid-stride. As I thought about my efforts to "fit in" to the Christian culture and be a disciple, the meaning of His words began to sink in. I tried so hard to say the right things, do the right things, and be appropriately "spiritual." Isn't that what Christianity and following Jesus is all about—being good?

No. Living as a disciple of Jesus is about receiving our relationship with God through faith in Jesus. It is about resting in Him and trusting in the salvation we received. It is about who we are, not what we do. We cannot rest without this understanding.

Deflated, but thankful for His revelation, I asked His forgiveness and asked Him to change me. He faithfully continues to change me over the years, and the fullness of my rest continues to deepen beyond what I ever thought possible. That idol sneaks in from time to time, but I have grown to recognize it more quickly, repent, and move on. Remember, nothing on our journey as a disciple is once and for all. The battle continues until the day we meet Jesus face to face.

Expecting God's Provision

Rest also means expecting God to take care of us when we obey Him.

Hebrews 4:9-10 tells us: "There remains, then, a Sabbath-rest for the people of God; for anyone who enters God's rest also rests from their works, just as God did from his."

If you turn back to Hebrews 3, you'll notice the author speaks of the Israelites whom Moses led out of Egypt—God said they would not enter His rest because of their disobedience. But for those who obeyed, He promised His rest. They could cease from their work and trust Him to provide all they needed. We can do the same. As we trust and obey Him, we can cease from our endless works and trust that He is enough for our salvation and He will provide all we need.

Here are a few more of God's encouraging promises to provide what we need, as a good Father:

> "Ask and it will be given to you; seek and you will find; knock and the door will be opened to you. For everyone who asks receives; the one who seeks finds; and to the one who knocks, the door will be opened. Which of you, if your son asks for bread, will give him a stone? Or if he asks for a fish, will give him a snake? If you, then, though you are evil, know how to give good gifts to your children, how much more will your Father in heaven give good gifts to those who ask him!."
>
> —Matthew 7:7-11

"Therefore I tell you, do not worry about your life, what you will eat or drink; or about your body, what you will wear. Is not life more than food, and the body more than clothes? Look at the birds of the air; they do not sow or reap or store away in barns, and yet your heavenly Father feeds them. Are you not much more valuable than they? Can any one of you by worrying add a single hour to your life?

And why do you worry about clothes? See how the flowers of the field grow. They do not labor or spin. Yet I tell you that not even Solomon in all his splendor was dressed like one of these. If that is how God clothes the grass of the field, which is here today and tomorrow is thrown into the fire, will he not much more clothe you—you of little faith? So do not worry, saying, 'What shall we eat?' or 'What shall we drink?' or 'What shall we wear?' For the pagans run after all these things, and your heavenly Father knows that you need them. But seek first his kingdom and his righteousness, and all these things will be given to you as well."
—Matthew 6:25-33

Staying Content with Where You Are

Continuing with the Israelites, rest also means staying content where we are and with what we have until God tells us to move, and then setting out when He tells us to go. It's about accepting what God brings and allows (manna) and not trying to get something else (meat) through complaining or demanding (Exodus 16). Paul also learned this valuable lesson, as he expressed in Philippians 4:12-13:

> I know what it is to be in need, and I know what it is to have plenty. I have learned the secret of being content in any and every situation, whether well fed or hungry, whether living in plenty or in want. I can do all this through him who gives me strength.

Again, it's about faithful obedience to God step by step, not about figuring things out or making things happen. It's about following Him, not our own plan.

And it's about thanksgiving. When we are content, our hearts overflow with thanksgiving to the One who can only give us good gifts.

> Every good and perfect gift is from above, coming down from the Father of the heavenly lights, who does not change like shifting shadows.
>   —James 1:17

The more we thank God for all He's provided, the more we stop comparing ourselves to others and wanting what they have. We're then free to enjoy what is right in front of us.

> This is the day which the Lord has brought about; we will rejoice and be glad in it.
>   —Psalm 118:24, AMPC

Trusting God Fully

Finally, to rest is to trust. Not just, "God is good all the time; all the time God is good" lip-service trust, but a "Yes, I'll obey even though what You said flies in the face of all logic and common sense" kind of trust. It's the Abraham level of trust which says, "Wherever you ask me to go, I'll go, and whatever you ask me to sacrifice or do, I'll do" (Hebrews 11:8-12, 17-19). This level of trust is not about us; it is all about God. As the song "Who Am I" by Casting Crowns says, it's because of Who God is and what He's done, not who we are or what we've done.

One of the best illustrations I've heard about complete and total trust is the story of a man who walked a tightrope over Niagara Falls. When he reached the other side, those waiting for him enthusiastically applauded his death-defying effort. He asked, "How many of you think I can do this again?" For a second time, he was eagerly cheered on. He then asked, "OK, so who wants to ride on my back?" Silence. Imagine that!

For an analytical person like me, trust isn't easy. But I've learned I can only rest to the degree that I trust God. My rest is directly proportional to how much I trust God in my heart.

I enjoy all types of puzzles. I enjoy the challenge of figuring out the answer. God created me with a logical mind that can usually get to the answer one way or another. When I can't figure it out, I know where to find the answer. Works great when pondering math problems, what to have for dinner, or who won last night's ball game. It even works when trying to figure out the ending to a movie or what's going to happen on the next episode of a TV series.

But it does not work with God. I know—I tried to apply the same analytical principles to figuring out God and making things happen when He was silent. I've worn myself out trying to stay one step ahead of God or trying to figure out where He's headed. Instead of finding answers, I wasted precious time.

When I moved to Raleigh in 1995 to live near my brother, I needed a job. Before I arrived, my brother gave me a lead from an advertisement he read. I called the place and they asked for my résumé. It seemed like the perfect job for me, so I immediately submitted my résumé and waited for them to contact me. Several weeks passed. By this time, I had moved and really needed to get to work. So, I prayed. God's answer: *Rest. Enjoy your time with your family—play with your niece and nephews.*

What? Do nothing? I remember thinking, *But I need a job.* Well-meaning family and friends thought so too—they coached me to apply for various jobs, send out résumés, call here, go there. In other words, I did the next practical thing that was in front of me. My anxiety and stress grew every day that passed without a response. Instead of fully enjoying the precious time with my family, I fretted over my lack of employment.

Three weeks later, I received a phone call asking me to come in for an interview. Who called? You guessed it: The very first place I sent a résumé. Someone quit and they needed a replacement quickly who had my specific skill set and experience. God provided a job for me at the perfect time, but I didn't trust Him enough to wait on Him. I was still trying to "do" what made sense.

I've also learned that resting in the Lord—wholly trusting in Him—is directly related to experiencing the peace of God.

Several years after I moved to Raleigh, I had a house for sale in Maryland. The Lord told me to do nothing: no realtor, just wait. As it sat with a "For Sale by Owner" sign for months, I had complete peace about following His orders. But others counseled me to get a realtor and just get it sold, if for no other reason than to stop making house payments.

As time went on and God stayed silent, I started to get restless. Did I really hear from God? When I prayed, I still had peace about doing nothing. But then I allowed reasoning to take over.

The advice from others—who also said they had prayed about it—was practical and reasonable, so I hired a realtor. Then I hired another realtor when the first didn't produce results after almost six months. With both, I had zero showings. Zero.

Eventually, the second realtor suggested putting the house up for auction. As I thought about it and prayed (in other words, explained to God why this was a good thing), I felt a huge relief that maybe I'd finally sell the house and be done with the whole process. Others agreed, so the auction was a go.

The house sold for a ridiculously low price, and I immediately regretted my decision. I realized my peace was gone—I moved instead of staying where God placed me—and the relief I felt had also vanished, crowded out by second-guessing that plagued my mind. But hey, no more house payments! I kept trying to talk myself into believing it was the right thing and justifying my decision with my own logic. I continued to pray and defend my position to God.

I lost my peace because I resorted to "doing" instead of resting in the Lord. I allowed my own reasoning and the opinions of others to guide me instead of Jesus. I was really, really sorry and confessed that to God every day, sometimes in tears. My peace started to return as I realized He had forgiven me, although I had no idea what to do next.

God was about to show me...and to give me a miracle.

I drove from Raleigh to Maryland the day of closing, despite the snowy, icy weather. After almost an hour of sitting in the attorney's waiting room, someone came out and said we'd need to close on another date because of a problem with the buyer's financing.

Immediately—and I mean right at that second—I knew in my heart that God had stopped the sale.

Despite my rebellion—yes, call it what it was—God intervened to save me from the consequences of my sin. He had other plans that I could never have foreseen, and the premature house sale didn't fit those plans. Humbled to the core, I cried almost all the way back to Raleigh...and laughed with intense joy at His goodness. God's plan for me—the reason He stopped that sale—was this: Almost two years later, I finally sold the house. Then at the Lord's direction (He guided me all the way and I obeyed this time), I bought a house that happened to be across the street from another house for sale. Don bought the other house. Yes, it's how I met my husband—a great God-story for another time (and one I shared more details about in my book, *Finding the Missing Something*).

Regaining Your Peace

God doesn't always intervene in our plans. Whether He does or doesn't, I always lose my peace and rest when I go my own way—when I seek temporary relief from painful or difficult circumstances. But I know how to regain my peace and enter back into His rest: repent and turn back to Jesus. He is the only source of true peace. In John chapters 14 through 16, Jesus counsels His disciples about how to live in a world that doesn't believe. Chapter 14 starts with Jesus telling His disciples to believe in Him:

> "Do not let your hearts be troubled. You believe in God; believe also in me."
> —John 14:1

And chapter 16 ends with Jesus telling His disciples to find peace in Him:

> "I have told you these things, so that in me you may have peace. In this world you will have trouble. But take heart! I have overcome the world."
> —John 16:33

"These things" that Jesus referred to include believing in Him, keeping His commands, showing you love Him by obeying Him, trusting Him, staying close to Him, and being willing to be hated by the world as He was hated.

When we fully rest in God alone, we have God's peace: the peace that passes all understanding and guards our hearts and minds in Christ Jesus (Philippians 4:7). His peace comes from a deep knowing and full acceptance that God is God, we are not; and His ways are always way better (and far higher) than ours (Isaiah 55:8-11).

So what does all this have to do with warfare? Remember, we've peeked at the back of the Book and know how the story ends...and Who won the war. Only by resting confidently in that victory, and by trusting in God's immeasurable love for us, can we fight wisely in His strength and not wear ourselves out fighting fruitless battles on our own. As we learn to increasingly rest in Him, we'll find ourselves increasingly able to recognize, and then defeat, whatever the enemy brings our way.

Dear Jesus,

*I struggle with resting when there is so much to be done. Help me to prioritize my life and time so You and I have more time together. Teach me to rest in the middle of chaos, and strengthen my faith to trust You with **all** that concerns me. Thank You for Your ultimate victory that assures my eternity with You. May I keep that in the forefront of my mind.*

In Your name I pray, Amen.

5

Facing Your Enemy, Not Fearing Him
(WARFARE)

What is your first instinct when something frightens you?

Maybe you heard a noise in your house in the middle of the night. Maybe someone whose behavior is unpredictable is walking toward you. Perhaps one of those ugly and disgusting camel crickets (a spider-like, ugly, brown creature) jumped on your chest while you were relaxing on the couch with a good book. Maybe you're afraid of heights and someone talked you into riding a roller-coaster. Or, could be one of your children—or grandchildren—hid and cried "boo!" at you as you rounded the corner.

Whatever the fearful event is, our first response in most cases is involuntary: panic grips our chest, we suck in a quick breath, and our body prepares its defense. Sometimes fear grips us so tightly we find ourselves rooted in place, paralyzed and barely breathing. Or we may lash out physically and verbally in reaction to the sudden shock of the event (and, for their sakes, hopefully the camel cricket or the "boo" crier can move faster than we can).

While we can't control this involuntary first response, we can absolutely control what we choose to do next. That next choice can vary widely, depending on what we understand and believe to be true about the object of our fear, and what we understand about the true meaning of "being safe."

Hundreds of times in the Bible, the Lord instructs us to not be afraid because He is with us. I always thought "do not be afraid" meant I should never *feel* afraid, even for an instant. But I realize that God meant we are to be courageous and not allow fear to stop us from enjoying life or from doing what He has commanded us to do. And what are His two greatest commandments? Love God with all your heart, mind, soul, and strength, and love your neighbor as yourself (Luke 10:27, Mark12:29-31).

What are some fears we must overcome to be able to walk in love? Fear of God's punishment, fear of the enemy, fear of getting hurt by others, and fear of what people will "get away with" if we forgive them.

Unhealthy Fear Revealed...and Healed

Early in my faith walk, I feared God. Not in the healthy, awesome, respectful way that's commanded when the Bible says "fear the Lord," but I feared God was out to punish me, and that eventually He'd reject me. He made me aware of this fear in a recurring dream.

In the middle of the night, I hear a noise. Cautiously, I rise and creep toward the bedroom door. Suddenly, a man appears in the doorway. I freeze to the spot. I see his feet first, then legs, then as my eyes move up his body, I notice his arms are raised. I don't look any further—not wanting to see the axe he holds, ready to strike me dead. Paralyzed with fear, I try to scream but nothing comes out.

Each time the dream occurred, I woke up sweating and frantic. *Whew, it was just a dream.*

After having that same dream repeatedly, I realized the Lord might be trying to tell me something. I prayed. *Lord, do I need to check my doors and windows before going to bed? Do I need to make sure I'm cautious when arriving home? Maybe I just need to stop reading suspense novels.*

Curious, I asked the Lord to show me the rest of the man I could never bear to look at in my dream. Much to my shock and dismay at having been afraid, it was *Him.* His arms were stretched forward to hug me, and He grinned from ear to ear. I couldn't believe it—I was *afraid* of God?

Yes. I felt threatened because I didn't have the whole picture. I feared Him because I didn't know Him. I thought I did because I read the Bible, went to church, and told others I loved Him. I realized from the dream that my love for Him, and my understanding of Him, were only skin deep. How could I trust someone to keep me safe if I feared him?

Learning to love and trust God is a process. As I spend more time with God and with others who love Him and love me, I begin to really *know* Him. The more

I know Him, the more I trust Him. The more I trust Him, the more I am able to receive His love. The more love I receive, the less I fear.

As I choose to let Him walk me through this process daily—it never ends—His perfect love casts out my fear (1 John 4:18). Only then can I even think about truly loving my neighbors and bringing God's Kingdom of love to them.

Who Is My Neighbor?

So, who, according to Jesus' instruction, is my neighbor?

In Luke 10:29, Jesus is asked that same question by an "expert in the law." In verses 30-35, Jesus answers with the parable of the Good Samaritan. After hearing the parable, the "expert in the law" correctly identifies the neighbor as the one who showed mercy to a person in need (verse 37). Loving a neighbor is not about being religious or being of the same culture or race, but about being merciful.

Given that parable, I am to be a neighbor to those who treat me unkindly. I am to show mercy to the miserable co-worker who is never satisfied and verbally takes it out on me. I am to smile and warmly greet the overworked person at the mall who is rude to me. I am to be kind to the angry protester who lashes out at me as I walk by. And yes, I am to pray for the thief who breaks into my house to steal all I have.

Wait, these sound more like enemies than neighbors. Maybe they are, but Jesus covers that, too. In Matthew 5:43-44, Jesus tells us to love our enemies and to pray for those who persecute us. In Romans 12:20, Paul tells us to feed and to clothe our enemies.

Yet Jesus also mentions *the* enemy, the devil: the thief who comes to steal, kill, and destroy (John 10:10)—the enemy who is out to keep us from all God has for us. In Luke 10:19, Jesus tells us, "I have given you authority to trample on snakes and scorpions and to overcome all the power of the enemy; nothing will harm you."

Seems confusing, doesn't it? How do we know who and when to overcome, and who and when to love? For the answer, we look back to Ephesians 6: our enemy—*the* enemy—is not flesh and blood, but spiritual powers of darkness led by the devil. So, we love *people*, and we overcome the spiritual powers of darkness that influence them.

We are never told to fear either of them, to avoid them, to ignore them, or to run from them. Both actions—loving and overcoming—require active participation on our part. It's difficult to participate unless we're facing them. Unless we are intentional with our words and actions, fear can sneak in.

Years ago, I had another extremely vivid dream.

Where am I?

This road I'm walking looks familiar, but it's way too dark to know for sure.

What's that up ahead? Flashing lights, cars crashed into each other, people screaming. Was there a car accident? Maybe I should go help...

Oh no, now I hear gun shots! What if the shooters come this way? I need to hide. NOW.

Good, here's a ditch. I'll just jump in and lay face down. They'll never see me here. I can't breathe, I can't move.

I'm scared...oomph, OH MY...what happened? The pain...I've been shot! They found me!

I've never been shot in real life, but the feeling was so intensely real I knew exactly what happened. I woke up in a sweat with my heart racing, thankful once again to be safely in my bed.

As I pondered and prayed about what the dream might mean, I had a thought so bold and clear I knew it was the Lord speaking to me: *Never, ever, turn your back on the enemy.*

We are fully equipped—with the armor of God, weapons of the Bible and prayer, and strength from resting in Jesus—to defeat anything that comes our way...as long as we are facing it. The armor covers our feet, our chests, and our heads. We have shields to hold in front of us, swords to swing, and prayers to declare. Facing our enemy, we can see to confidently defeat him. Running leaves us vulnerable to attack and injury, and robs us of the victory Jesus already won for us.

Setting People Free

One of my favorite Bible stories is in Mark 5:1-20—the healing of an out-of-control, demon-possessed man.

He lived in the tombs and cried out day and night, most certainly feared by all who heard and saw him. Jesus, however, was not afraid of him because He could see beyond the man's actions to the impure spirits that controlled him. And Jesus knew that God's power and authority were greater than those spirits. In God's power and authority, Jesus commanded the impure spirits to leave the man. At the end of the story, the man was found dressed and in his right mind.

Because of the power and authority we have in Jesus, we are to do the same thing He did: Set people free. Our opportunities may not seem as dramatic as the one in this story, but they are just as important. For example, when we encounter an angry person and make *that person* our enemy by responding in anger, we aid and abet the devil in his attempt to harm the one Jesus calls our neighbor. Instead, the power of the Holy Spirit enables us to see beyond the actions to the person who needs mercy. We can see the true enemy who holds our neighbor captive with lies and power. And we can show that person love and mercy.

But wait. Angry people sometimes lash out in their anger. And needy, wounded people can be hurtful with their words and actions. Is it safe to reach out in love? We could get wounded ourselves.

Yes, it's possible and often probable we'll be hurt as we move forward without, or in spite of, fear. We are fighting very real battles. The term "being safe" does not mean we won't get wounded. Remember John 16:33—we'll have trouble in this world. Yet, despite anything man can do to us, God is always with us (Matthew 1:23; 28:20). He will never leave us or forsake us (Joshua

1:5; Deuteronomy 31:8). He sustains us and helps us through whatever circumstances we face (Psalm 18:35; 54:4; 55:22). We are always safe in His protection (Psalm 91).

Now, if you are in a dangerous or abusive situation, please get help. I'm not advocating that anyone should stay in a situation that is physically, emotionally, or mentally dangerous. I'm talking about the spiritual battles we fight in day-to-day encounters with the angry clerk, unfriendly neighbor, and other imperfect people living alongside us in this fallen world.

When we do get hurt, we have the opportunity to choose one of the greatest activators of God's love: forgiveness. We can forgive those who hurt, perse-cute, lash out at, and betray us. We don't have to *feel* like forgiving them. We don't have to tell the one we're forgiving that we've done so unless God directs us to do so. Often, we will still feel hurt or angry. Fully experi-encing forgiveness—no more hurt or anger—is a process that takes time. It starts with our choice to forgive and continues to completion with ongoing choices to keep forgiving (Matthew 18:21-22).

Why Forgive?

Forgiving someone despite how we feel is not hypo-critical; it's obedient. Jesus commands us to forgive, and He never commands us to do something we cannot do. By the power of the Holy Spirit, we can forgive as Jesus forgave us. Once we forgive, we can allow Jesus to love that person through us by choosing to be kind, gentle, merciful, and praying for the one who hurt us.

In Ephesians 4, Paul writes to us about unity in the body of Christ. He ends with this command in verse 32 that summarizes the chapter and holds the key to being unified in Christ: "Be kind and compassionate to one another, forgiving each other, just as in Christ God forgave you."

Just as important as extending forgiveness to others is receiving Jesus' forgiveness fully and deeply when we've repented and turned from our own sins. By faith, we can believe our righteousness is fully restored and we are made new, as John reminds us:

> If we confess our sins, he is faithful and just and will forgive us our sins and purify us from all unrighteousness.
> —1 John 1:9

We don't need to fear punishment from Him even when we face consequences; He disciplines those He loves (Hebrews 12:4-6). We don't need to beat ourselves up when we do something we "knew better" not to do. If we don't receive His forgiveness when we confess— maybe we think we need to pay in some way because the sin was so bad—we are basically saying, "What you did, Jesus, is not good enough. I need to pay for my own sin."

Sobering, isn't it?

Forgiveness is a choice, and it's a process. It's not a feeling. It's a command from God with serious consequences for disobedience:

For if you forgive people their trespasses [their reckless and willful sins, leaving them, letting them go, and giving up resentment], your heavenly Father will also forgive you.

But if you do not forgive others their trespasses [their reckless and willful sins, leaving them, letting them go, and giving up resentment], neither will your Father forgive you your trespasses.

—Matthew 6:14-15, AMPC

We need not fear what a person might do when we forgive or what they might "get away with" if they never apologize, change their behavior, or are sorry for what they did. Our responsibility is obedience: forgive as we have been forgiven and without limit (Matthew 18:21-35). The consequences of others' actions are not our responsibility. Our time might be better spent considering our own consequences if we refuse to forgive.

Sadly, both parties are not always willing to move forward in forgiveness. When that happens, be assured you are always forgiven by God when you confess. Learn from what happened. Apologize if you've wronged the other person and continue to pray for that person. Forgive the one who hurt you, even if they don't ask. The relationship may never be the same, but you can enjoy God's peace when you do as much as possible to live in peace with others (Romans 12:18).

Don't Stay Stuck on What You Can't Change

God showed me an analogy of how the enemy operates to keep us stuck in the past. Picture driving a car. Most of the time, our eyes are on the road in front of us. As needed, we glance in the rearview mirror to see who is behind us. If we spent all our time intently looking in the rearview mirror as we drove, we'd likely run into something…or we'd have to stop the car.

That's what our enemy tries to do—get us so focused on what happened in the past we can't move forward. When that happens, we can keep forgiving, keep our eyes on Jesus, and set our hearts on what God has in front of us.

With our armor (identity) securely in place, we are eternally protected by Jesus—we are safe and secure in His 24/7/365-presence. We are equipped with all we need to love people and to battle the dark spiritual forces on their behalf. When we love in the face of hate, bless in the face of cursing, and forgive as Jesus forgave us, Jesus' perfect love is activated and fear is cast out.

Dear Jesus,

I confess I'm often afraid of getting hurt, so I won't speak up or reach out. Give me Your eyes to see my circumstances and the people in my life. Teach me to remember that You have me covered always. Give me courage to reach out in kindness, no matter what might happen.

In Your name I pray, Amen.

6

Audible—The Power of the Spoken Word
(WARF**A**RE)

"**D**addy, look at that car over there!" My nephew screamed at his dad, my brother Mike, who was sitting right next to him in the truck.

Laughing, Mike replied, "Didn't hear you, Tim, could you say it a little louder?"

"DADDY, LOOK AT THAT CAR OVER THERE!"

Tim didn't understand Mike's tone of voice to know his dad was only joking. His three-year-old brain heard, "Say it louder," so he took the words at face value and did just as his dad asked.

How many times have our words been taken out of context or subtle tones missed, causing misunderstandings between us and others? I've often heard, "It's not the words you said, but *how* you said them."

To a point, that's true. John tells us to, "Speak the truth *in love*." We don't need to shout it or shove it at people. We can "feed" it to them in a way they'll receive and ingest it.

In the context of spiritual warfare, though, the actual words we speak make *all* the difference.

Just as my nephew did, the enemy takes our words at face value. But he doesn't do it innocently. Our enemy is legalistic and remembers everything for the purpose of using our own words against us. That's the focus of this chapter: the power of the spoken word.

Through His Word, God instructs us that what we speak brings consequences, good or bad. In Proverbs 12:18, we read: "The words of the reckless pierce like swords, but the tongue of the wise brings healing." Other verses instruct us regarding our speech, like Ephesians 4:15, which tells us to speak the truth in love. Most importantly, we are instructed to *speak*. *Audibly*, not just in our minds.

The spoken word is powerful.

God *spoke* the world into existence.

The Old Testament prophets *spoke* God's truth, judgment, and warnings to the people so they'd repent from their sin and turn back to God.

Jesus *spoke* truth to the people about Himself, God, and their sinful condition so they'd know Who He was and understand His great love for them.

Paul, Peter, Stephen, and others *spoke* truth about Jesus so people would repent and turn to Jesus for salvation.

Throughout Scripture, God and people *spoke* and things happened. They didn't quietly think to themselves, they opened their mouths and released audible words. Their spoken words wielded power. Did they yell or speak with great emotion? Perhaps, at times. But the volume wasn't the key: it was the words they chose to use and the authority behind those words. One thing I've noticed in the gospels is the absence of adverbs. We read "Jesus said," often, but not "Jesus said *strongly* (or *sorrowfully* or *angrily* or *softly*)." *How* He spoke was not important; the words He chose said all that needed to be said.

The spoken word is powerful, but not all power is good.

The Power of Life or Death

In James 3:3-10, James talks about the tongue and teaches us that life and death are in the power of the tongue (verse 8). When we speak truth, and speak what God gives us to speak, His life-giving power is released to heal, encourage, and restore. When we speak lies, slander, gossip, or angry and unkind words, the enemy's power is released to steal, kill, and destroy.

Ephesians 4:29, one of my life verses, says, "Do not let any unwholesome talk come out of your mouths, but only what is helpful for building others up according to their needs, that it may benefit those who listen." Here are a few of many verses that exhort us about the words we speak:

Therefore each of you must put off falsehood and speak truthfully to your neighbor, for we are all members of one body.
—Ephesians 4:25

Brothers and sisters, do not slander one another. Anyone who speaks against a brother or sister or judges them speaks against the law and judges it. When you judge the law, you are not keeping it, but sitting in judgment on it.
—James 4:11

But now you must also rid yourselves of all such things as these: anger, rage, malice, slander, and filthy language from your lips.
—Colossians 3:8

In every one of these verses, we are not told to "think about it," "pray about it," or "get counsel about it." We're not told, "try to." We're told to *do* it! Because God never tells us to do something we are not able to do by the power of His Holy Spirit, we must have the ability to control what we speak.

What we speak is our choice. Therefore, it is our choice to release the power of life or death into every interaction with another person. Jesus warns us about the importance of words in this sobering verse:

But I tell you that men will have to give account on the day of judgment for every careless word they have spoken.
—Matthew 12:36

In other translations, the word *careless* is written as "idle" or "useless." In other words, if a word does not bear fruit, we don't need to speak it.

Wow, how sobering is that? Most of us know the difference between truth and lies. But how often do we speak careless words that we want to take back, sometimes right after the words leave our mouths?

Recently, the Lord used an interesting verse to convict me about the quick and careless words I spoke.

> Do not continue offering or yielding your bodily members [and faculties] to sin as instruments (tools) of wickedness. But offer and yield yourselves to God as though you have been raised from the dead to [perpetual] life, and your bodily members [and faculties] to God, presenting them as implements of righteousness.
> —Romans 6:13, AMPC

For me, the first "bodily member" that came to mind was my mouth. It's so tempting for me to speak negatively about people and circumstances, or to complain when things don't go as I plan or how I think they should go. Especially at work, opportunities to get caught up in the moment are plentiful. And I can be very quick to respond to whatever is going on—sometimes good, sometimes not so good. The day the Lord brought this verse to my attention, I indeed had many opportunities to be tested. Here are just a few:

- I received a call at work from my apartment manager, then launched into a complaint about the complex to my co-workers. I immediately saw this verse in my mind, so I added something positive and moved on.

- Someone complained about a situation, and I started to join in. But again, the verse came to mind and I stopped short.
- I heard a conversation about someone who used to work with us but left the company, and I joined in with the critics before I could stop myself. Once again, God used the verse to help me stop talking and walk away.

All day, I battled over my words. And all day, the verse kept coming to my mind as a reminder. Sometimes I choked back the wrong words in time, sometimes they slipped out.

Thinking Before Speaking

Even now, the Lord continues to use this verse to keep me aware of—and help me change—a very bad habit of speaking without thinking. Here are other examples of areas where we may be likely to use careless words:

- Using common phrases and idioms without giving a second thought to the actual meaning of the words we're speaking. In a teaching I heard about words, the speaker brought up these examples of careless statements: "I just love him to death," or, "She just tickles me to death." Another one is, "I'll kill you if you tell anyone about this." Will you really?
- Making a commitment with our words, then not following through. Do you make vows and

promises without thinking about what it will take to fulfill them? When we don't keep our word, we weaken relationships by breaking trust. It could be something as simple as, "I'll call you later," and not calling. Or it could be, "I'll always be there for you," and then circumstances change and make that impossible.

- Sharing someone's personal information when asking someone else to pray for them. Before we even think about what we're saying, we've shared confidential information. When word gets back to them, they can feel betrayed.

- Passing along something we heard about someone as truth. We form an opinion about the person based on what we heard. Then we find out it's not true at all.

- Agreeing with friends or family members when they put down someone who wronged them. It's easy to take sides; but we are called to be peacemakers, not strife stirrers.

- Forecasting what *could* happen out of fear or another emotion, without thinking. ("They are not going to like that." "I'm so afraid he'll fail that test." "She's going to struggle with that all her life.") Again, these words give the enemy power to influence the outcome—he'll whisper lies related to what we spoke, and we'll start to believe them, and so will others.

Included in careless words are those little white lies we sometimes use to avoid hurting others or to protect them. We justify it by saying it's for their own good.

But they often find out the truth despite our efforts. Then they may not trust us to be truthful in the future. Only God can protect us; and when we lie, we remove ourselves from His protection. What we are really saying is, "I don't trust you can fix this (help them, get us past this, preserve our relationship) anyway, what they don't know, won't hurt them."

When we use careless words, trust is broken. People are hurt. Relationships are damaged, sometimes seriously. Most of all, death is spoken instead of life, and power is given to our enemy to tear down instead of to God to build up.

Learning and understanding the *right* choice—the *life* choice—is a process. We do not naturally speak life-giving words, or even know what they are in many cases. Often, we start our relationships with Jesus while still entrenched in worldly ways and words. That was me, for sure!

Learning a New Way to Speak

I began my journey as a disciple of Jesus in my 30s after living and working in the world's culture for many years. To say my vocabulary needed work would be an understatement. After I relayed something that happened at work to a friend, using somewhat colorful language, he said, "You know, your language doesn't fit who you are as a disciple. You need to pray about your words."

That was just the beginning. I also gossiped quite a bit and spewed hurtful words when I felt hurt or angry. I needed to learn a different way of speaking by learning and obeying Jesus' commands regarding my words. I needed—and still need—to develop the fruit of self-control over my mouth. It's an ongoing process, one that I need to intentionally commit myself to follow every day. To engage in the process of change is always a choice.

Letting God Fine-Tune Your Words

Recently during my quiet time, about a week after I read Romans 6:13, the Lord gave me another life-changing revelation. This time it was on the infamous James passage about the tongue:

> With the tongue we praise our Lord and Father, and with it we curse human beings, who have been made in God's likeness. Out of the same mouth come praise and cursing. My brothers and sisters, this should not be.
>
> —James 3:9-10

In God's fine-tuning of my words, He showed me cursing isn't always overt, loud, or angry. He revealed to me a series of questions I can ask myself about all I write, speak, and even think.

Is what I'm about to write or speak going to…

…build up or tear down?
…encourage or discourage?
…praise or cut down?
…bring laughter, but at someone else's expense?
…sound witty or cutting?

...promote unity or breed strife?
...make peace or incite war?
...make someone laugh or hurt their feelings/
  mock them?
...bring honor or disrespect?
...foster trust or spread gossip?

Quite a list, isn't it? I don't know about you, but regrettably I have days where I spend way more time on the right side of that list than on the left side.

God showed me that the "ors" in my list are cursing—bringing death with my words instead of speaking life. I can share two hours of awesome God stories with someone and invalidate it in a quick minute with careless cursing.

Granted, our lives are about God and not about us or about "getting it right." But we are called to bring Him glory and honor and to witness to His goodness. How can we do that when we curse, sometimes more than we praise?

> The tongue has the power of life and death, and those who love it will eat its fruit.
> —Proverbs 18:21

It's Our Responsibility

Regardless of where we are in the transformation process, we are still responsible for every word that comes out of our mouths. We have the power to choose what to speak and what to hold back. What we choose directly impacts the outcome of each encounter we have with another person.

One day after church, God showed me how His power and grace are activated by my choice to speak kind words instead of speaking out of the anger I felt.

Someone did something I felt was grossly inconsiderate. As I approached the person, words of anger and judgment fermented inside at the perceived injustice I had suffered. Ready to let loose, I heard God whisper, *Ask how she's doing today.*

What? Be *nice?* Are you *kidding* me—after what she did?

Somehow, despite my feelings, I chose to obey. As soon as I started the question, "How are you…" *all* feelings of anger left, and my heart filled with compassion. I barely heard what she said because I was so awestruck at what the Lord did in my heart in an instant. I did hear enough to know that my perceptions about the offense were totally wrong—she had had a very rough week, and I didn't know it. One choice to obey was all it took for the Lord to miraculously save me from myself and from possibly hurting someone more than they were already hurting.

Sometimes we exercise self-control by *not* speaking. Silence is often the better option when our emotions bubble up and the words screaming to be released would be bleeped out in a G-rated movie. Before speaking, we can ask the Lord to put a guard over our mouths (Psalm 141:3). We can count to ten (yes, that really works). We can be slow to speak and quick to listen (James 1:19-20).

Whatever words we choose are just that: our choice. The Bible leaves no room for debate about that—we can exercise our free will any way we choose, including what we speak.

It's not about being perfect, though. Paul says in Romans 7:

> I do not understand what I do. For what I want to do I do not do, but what I hate I do. And if I do what I do not want to do, I agree that the law is good. As it is, it is no longer I myself who do it, but it is sin living in me. For I know that good itself does not dwell in me, that is, in my sinful nature. For I have the desire to do what is good, but I cannot carry it out. For I do not do the good I want to do, but the evil I do not want to do— this I keep on doing.
>
> —Romans 7:15-19

He also provides the answer: Jesus!

> So I find this law at work: Although I want to do good, evil is right there with me. For in my inner being I delight in God's law; but I see another law at work in me, waging war against the law of my mind and making me a prisoner of the law of sin at work within me. What a wretched man I am! Who will rescue me from this body that is subject to death? Thanks be to God, who delivers me through Jesus Christ our Lord!
>
> —Romans 7:21-25

With Jesus, we have hope. Just as our careless or hurtful words bring death, words of forgiveness, mercy, and kindness can redeem what the enemy has stolen when both parties are willing to confess and forgive. Once you've confessed your sin to God, apologize to the person you hurt. Your gentle apology can calm their wrath, and change the atmosphere.

Changing the Atmosphere

I once experienced this atmosphere change in a powerful way when I chose to apologize to Don. The Lord showed me I was sinning against Don by not submitting to him—I didn't trust him to lead or protect me. The atmosphere in our house was tense, sometimes so thick you could cut it with a knife. Remember my story in the awareness chapter about how demons can surround and influence due to unforgiveness? Add unconfessed sin to that list.

One morning, I made the decision to submit to Don—to trust him in my heart—but didn't get a chance to confess until later. Only when I spoke my apology and we prayed out loud did the atmosphere in our house change. The enemy's hold was broken and God's peace flooded our home.

Remember that your apology, forgiveness, and changed actions won't always bring reconciliation or restoration to relationships. Others have the same freedom of choice that you do, and they can use that freedom to hold a grudge or continue to speak lies. You are only accountable to the Lord for your own choices, so focus on them. Change what you can, pray as the Lord leads, and place that relationship in God's hands.

Our enemy is not all-knowing—he can't read our minds. But he's a master at reading body language and facial expressions and will bombard us with condemnation and lies when it appears we are down. We battle him by speaking truth out loud, even when we don't feel like it. The more truth we speak, the more our countenance will change, and the more strength we'll have, the less hold the enemy will have on us.

You've heard, the advice, "think before you speak," right? That advice is very helpful, like counting to ten. I have a sign on my office wall with suggestions for questions to ask yourself during those ten seconds before you speak:

> T – is it true?
> H – is it helpful?
> I   – is it inspiring?
> N – is it necessary?
> K – is it kind?

I think I need to have this tattooed on the back of my hand!

Choosing to Praise

Finally, you can make your words powerful and life-giving when you praise and worship. Not just listening to the music or reading the Bible, but singing or speaking the words out loud. When we praise God, we remind ourselves of Who He is—we magnify Him. When we magnify Him, the enemy's lies become more visible and problems seem more manageable. Our minds are renewed and our souls are refreshed.

When you are battling illness, or if you're discouraged, defeated, or angry, choose to speak praises to God from a favorite Psalm in Scripture. Or sing a favorite worship chorus about how awesome He is. Instruct yourself about the majesty of God and remind anyone or anything listening that He is holy, all-powerful, loving, and most of all, He is your Daddy.

Dear Jesus,

Oh my, do I need help here! Help me to listen better and speak more slowly. Put a guard over my mouth that I might not sin against You. Change my heart so that my words become more like Your words. May the words of my heart and the meditations of my heart be pleasing to You. Thank You for Your Word that is full of instruction on how we should speak.

In Your name I pray, Amen.

7

Rejoicing in the Lord Always (WARFA**R**E)

Paul begins the last section of his letter to the Philippians with a powerful verse:

> Rejoice in the Lord always. I will say it again: Rejoice!
> —Philippians 4:4

Paul believed rejoicing is so important he repeated the word.

As I pondered this verse, two key points caught my attention. The first is the word itself, *rejoice*. From *Dictionary.com*, *rejoice* means:

- to be glad; take delight (often followed by in): "to rejoice in another's happiness."
- to make joyful; gladden: "a song to rejoice the heart."

Rejoicing as a Response to Blessing and Miracles

The first definition describes our action, like in the verse. It's easy to rejoice in response to…

> …a new job or a promotion,
> …the birth of a child or grandchild,
> …a successful surgery or recovery from illness, and
> …birthdays, holidays, weddings, and graduations.

Most of us have many reasons to rejoice and be thankful. We're excited and uplifted when we celebrate our accomplishments. We gather together with family and friends to share each other's joys. We laugh, eat (usually too much), sing, and congratulate our loved ones on their successes.

We also rejoice when we see God move in someone's life or in a situation. Have you ever prayed for someone who was healed and delivered on the spot, or been miraculously healed yourself? I have. The emotions of overwhelming joy and amazement are indescribable.

On one particular occasion, I spent the day hiking with a friend who had asked many questions about Jesus. She had also shared about past experiences with a cult-like group. When we went to my house after the hike, I brought out my Bible (and one for her) so she could read about Jesus for herself.

As I started talking, I noticed her facial expression tighten up like she was in severe pain. I offered the Bible to her so she could read something along with me. She refused and jerked away from it like it was poisonous and would bite her if she got too close. I confidently told her about Jesus' power and how He is greater than anything or anyone else. The more I talked about Him, the more she doubled over in pain, grabbing her head as though it would explode if she didn't hold it together.

"What's wrong?" I asked.

"I've got a killer headache. It won't stop. I can't focus. And I can't touch that Bible!" she responded.

"Can I put my hands on your head and pray for your headache?"

Pause.

"Okay, but it won't help," she said.

I leaned over and gently placed both hands on her head.

"Headache, be gone in Jesus' name! Thank you, Lord, for Your healing power."

The moment I started to pray—I mean that very moment—she looked up, startled and amazed. I removed my hands after finishing my prayer, and she slowly sat back.

"What's wrong now?" I asked.

"Nothing. Wow. My headache is completely gone."

God gave us a tangible healing miracle! Inside I gleefully jumped up and down, rejoicing in my spirit (OH MY, IT WORKED!). Outside, I calmly said, "That's because Jesus has *all* power and *all* authority. And He loves you." We spent the next hour or so reading the Bible together, which was also miraculous given she had not been able to get near it without severe pain only moments before. We both tearfully rejoiced in God's miraculous healing and in His goodness. That night marked the beginning of her walk with Jesus.

On another occasion, I received healing for a cyst on my wrist. At a prayer meeting, I mentioned I had a doctor's appointment to have him look at the cyst. The group prayed for it, and one of the women confidently declared God was healing it. She instructed me to thank God for the healing every day and bless my wrist, in faith. Feeling doubt but wanting to believe, I felt God gave me permission to cancel my doctor's appointment for that afternoon, then I prayed as she instructed.

After about a week I noticed it looked smaller. Then one day, I looked down and it was completely gone. It hasn't come back. Yes, and amen! Another time of rejoicing in God's healing.

While God healed my hand supernaturally, He has often used doctors to bring healing. I've had minor surgeries, been on medication, and changed my diet at a doctor's direction, and the healing I received was just as tangible as God's direct healing. God gets to choose the healing method, we step out in faith toward where He leads.

Rejoicing for the good gifts and healing we receive pleases God. He wants us to be thankful and appreciative when He heals us and blesses us. He takes delight in us and loves it when we appreciate His goodness. But that's not the full meaning of "rejoicing in the Lord."

Rejoicing in Who He Is...
and in Who We Are in Him

In Luke 10, Jesus' disciples are sent on a mission to heal the sick, cast out demons, and proclaim the Kingdom of God. They come back amazed (verse 17) (perhaps similar to how I felt about the instant healing of my friend's headache). They probably expected a high-five from Jesus, with His congratulations on a job well done.

Jesus does affirm what they experienced (verses 18-19), but then He cautions them: "Do not rejoice that the spirits submit to you, but rejoice that your names are written in heaven" (verse 20).

In other words, Jesus was saying…

Rejoice because you are Mine, not because of what you can do for Me.

Rejoice because you are Mine for eternity, not because of what you did for Me in one moment.

Rejoice in the life I give you, not in what you do with that life.

Notice that Philippians 4:4 says to rejoice *in* the Lord. It's not about us, or anything in us, or anything we can do. Jesus is our focus and the object of our rejoicing. This enables us to rejoice *in* the Lord even when things aren't going well, like when we…

   …lose our job,
   …get a bad medical report,
   …lose a loved one, or
   …struggle with relationships, finances, or other
      difficult circumstances.

To rejoice *in* the Lord means to turn our focus away from the circumstances and toward the One who can make us joyful in the midst of suffering. As our Comforter (2 Corinthians 1), He knows much of our comfort comes from focusing on Him and Who He is. He hasn't left or forsaken us; He is still in control, and He loves us with an everlasting love. His Spirit rejoices in us when we're in the midst of pain—simultaneously praising God and crying out the pain of a broken heart. We have the unique privilege of being able to feel deep joy and sorrow at the same time—peace in the storm.

I remember a difficult work situation I endured for several months. I had to work closely with someone I didn't want to see at all. For two months, I begged the Lord to remove me from the situation. Finally, He responded with these words to my heart: *Three more months.*

Fine.

One day I felt particularly feisty and rebellious during my morning prayer time. I chose to pray anyway.

"Okay, Lord, You said I need to be thankful in *all* things. I'm not feeling it, but here goes. I'm thankful I have a job. I'm thankful I have to work with this person I don't want to see. I'm thankful I have to do this for three more months, even though I want to leave now. I'm thankful You've asked me to do the impossible."

Pause.

"Whatever. Amen."

Off to work I went, surrounded by a swirling cloud of anger, but playing worship music and trying to rejoice. Through gritted teeth, I chose to pray, albeit with quite an attitude. I didn't feel any peace, only anger and frustration. But I kept speaking the truth.

It turned out to be one of the best days I ever had.

Everything I touched was successful. The co-worker I wanted to avoid helped me with a tough task and behaved kindly toward me. Humbled, I cried all the way home. God's kindness did indeed lead me to repentance.

"God, I'm so sorry for being such a brat and for acting so rebelliously. I really do love You. Thank You for being so understanding and forgiving. Please help me to trust You more."

Choosing to Rejoice

As you saw from my story, rejoicing isn't about how you feel. It's about what you choose to do. It's not about the state of your emotions, it's about the attitude of your heart. Are you facing God or turned away from Him? Are you choosing to obey regardless of how you feel? When I did, I experienced His peace and joy in the midst of my difficulty.

Do you remember the second definition of rejoice? It's to "make joyful; gladden." That's what the Lord does for us when we choose to rejoice in Him regardless of how we feel or what we see. I believe my choice to pray and worship—to obey—opened the door for God to work in my life that day. Nothing on the outside changed. I still had to go to work every day and face that person. I did not get my way; instead, I received the blessing of God's joy, presence, and provision when I chose to go *His* way.

At the end of three months, I was more than ready to go. But alas, it wasn't time yet, I heard "three more months" again! In His wisdom, the Lord knew that if He told me the whole timeframe in the beginning, the discouragement would have tempted me to take matters into my own hands. He wanted to teach me how to rejoice in Him as I waited. I made more mistakes along the way, but His joy and peace returned every time I chose to praise Him and be thankful, no matter what.

More importantly, His plan was for me to move to Raleigh, NC and not back to Maryland. My brother had to move to Raleigh first because it wasn't a place where I knew anyone, and he didn't move there until August…a full eight months after I started asking God to move me.

Why Raleigh? It's where I met Don, my husband, five years later.

Rejoicing as thanksgiving *to* the Lord is about what He's done for or given to us. He delights in giving us good gifts, and He delights in our appreciation of those gifts. We recognize Him as the source of our happy times, and that's a good thing.

Rejoicing *in* the Lord is about magnifying the One who is faithful *in* all circumstances. It's a celebration of Who God is, not what He does for us. Rejoicing *in* the Lord enables us to endure and embrace whatever comes our way, knowing He is with us and for us. It changes our focus from our circumstances to our God.

Some days it takes every ounce of our will to lift our hands and hearts in praise. Those are usually the days we need it the most.

When we praise God *just because He's God* it lifts our spirits. We love on Him. We bless Him. We declare Who He is and how much He loves us. We marvel at His creation. We declare and thank Him for His attributes:

Provider, Healer, Counselor, Prince of Peace, Almighty God, Everlasting Father…just to name a few.

When we rejoice *in* the Lord, we regain perspective on our purpose in life and on who He created us to be. We realize our enemy has already been defeated and has no authority in our lives. We can experience peace and joy regardless of what is going on around us.

Our God is amazing. Let's take a few moments and rejoice in Him together. Let's enter His gates with thanksgiving and His courts with praise (Psalm 100:4). Remember the last chapter? Praise him audibly… starting with today's prayer:

Dear Jesus,

Thank you that Your joy is my strength (Nehemiah 8:10).

Thank you that You are my strength and shield, and You help me when I trust in You (Psalm 28:7).

Thank you that You will never leave me or forsake me (Joshua 1:5).

Thank you that You are my rock, my fortress, my deliverer (2 Samuel 22:2, Psalm 18:2, Psalm 62:2).

Thank you that You are my salvation (Exodus 15:2, Psalm 118:21, Isaiah 12:2).

Thank you for Your great love and faithfulness (Psalm 117:2, Lamentations 3:23, Psalm 108:4).

Thank you that You are merciful and forgiving (Daniel 9:9, 1 John 1:9).

In Your name I pray, Amen.

8

Entertainment, or Exposure to Temptation?
(WARFARE)

You may be thinking: *How does my entertainment affect my ability to love others?*

Romans 8:2 instructs us to, "not conform to the pattern of this world, but be transformed by the renewing of your mind." I think we can agree that what we "take in" directly impacts our thoughts, and what we "think on" affects our words and our behavior. Let's look at how our entertainment choices can start us down a path that can pollute our hearts, thereby affecting our ability to love.

The lyrics of a popular children's song by Zondervan Music Publishers, titled "O Be Careful Little Eyes" (1956), cautions children to be careful what they see and what they hear because their Father above is looking down on them in love. Additional verses caution children to be careful what their little hands do, where their little feet go, what their little tongues say, who their little hearts trust, and what their little minds think.

Casting Crowns added depth to this simple song to create an adult version titled, "Slow Fade." The lyrics caution adults to be careful with what they see and where they go because change doesn't happen in a single day, but slowly over time. The song recognizes that it's not generally one big action that causes us to give in to temptation, but a series of small actions that lead us away from God, and then each other, misstep by misstep. (You can listen to the song on YouTube, search for Casting Crowns Slow Fade.)

Culture Drives our Entertainment Choices

These songs come to mind when I think about choosing entertainment and activities. We all need entertainment—time away from our busy schedules to refresh our souls. Reading a good book, going for a hike in the woods, watching a good movie, building a puzzle, attending a sporting event—we have as many choices as there are different types of people. Decades ago, we could flip on the TV and channel surf through wholesome selections of family entertainment. We could go to the theatre and see most of the movies without worrying that we'd see objectionable content. We could pick up magazines at the grocery store and skim through the pages.

Now?

We live in a culture in which many movies, TV shows, books, and songs or music videos are riddled with half-naked women, sex, violence, and coarse language. TV shows depict men, especially fathers, as weak and stupid. Comedy routines mock and ridicule people who are different. Songs glorify violence, drugs, divorce, and illicit sex while mocking church, God, and honor. Books that glorify abuse and bullying become bestsellers that are made into movies.

On all fronts, the names of God and Jesus are used in vain and in anger. And if we aren't careful, we may eventually begin to think and act this way, as well.

Sadly, there's a huge market for sinful media in our culture. Even when we are careful with our choices, we live in a world full of godless sights and sounds. Have you ever been watching a wholesome TV show and had to turn away to avoid offensive commercials? It's increasingly difficult to be "in the world" (be witnesses, make disciples) and not "of it". (John 15:18-20 says we are no longer "of this world" once we are His). The enemy tempts us from all directions, around the clock, with the intention of filling us with live grenades he can detonate later at his whim.

Yes, wholesome choices are still available, but it takes a lot more effort and intention to find them.

When we see images, they are imprinted on our brains. The same thing is true for what we read because words create images and stir emotions. What do the words lead us to do? Do they uplift or tear down? Do they invoke feelings of lust and anger, or stir us to compassion and prayer? Do they make us think about and ponder God and being closer to Him, or make us want to put on a fig leaf?

I know this sounds trite, but, if you can't picture Jesus enjoying it with you, don't do it.

Listening for God's Whisper

Sometimes what to take in—or not—is obvious. Do you ever feel dirty or uncomfortable while watching or reading something that contains violence, sex, evil, or other ungodly content? That's conviction. The Lord's spirit is whispering to your conscience. Other times we may find ourselves far away from the path we know is right and wonder how we got there—maybe we responded to some of the Lord's nudges and ignored others. Little by little, one choice at a time, we lose our sensitivity to His voice. The enemy's goal is to get us to turn down the volume of our conscience until his lies and our own fleshly lusts are louder than God's voice, and make us too weak to resist Satan's temptations.

The world is full of good and evil. How can you tell what is evil? Many people use the word "God" when they talk about spiritual power. Isn't that good? Not always. If the source of the power is not Jesus, it is of the devil. There is no middle ground. When people claim to be spiritual but don't claim Jesus as Lord and Savior, they are being guided and often deceived by demonic forces. Jesus Himself said He is the Way, the Truth, and the Life, and no one comes to the Father (God) except through Him (John 14:6).

That's another way Satan lures us away from Jesus: he tempts us to follow and believe in the good of other "spiritual" paths. TV shows and movies about "good" witches, magic, paranormal activity, and the occult are increasingly popular. Fortune telling, psychics, and practices like feng shui tempt us to seek knowledge about the future or peace from other sources. God wants us trusting Him with our future, not anyone or anything else. He is a jealous God (Exodus 34:14) who doesn't want us being led astray.

These things, including fortune telling, are not harmless to us. How can psychics know so much about people and be seemingly accurate with their predictions? Remember that the enemy is an expert at body language, and that demons are surrounding us all the time. They whisper to the psychics and tell them about us. Even if we seek their counsel just for amusement, when we listen to what they say to us, we are taking in words that have the power to lead us astray. Even games about the occult—such as Ouija boards expose us to the forces of darkness that can make us expose us more susceptible to Satan's lies and deceit. Each step in that direction leads us away from trusting in God's love and empowering truth.

Focusing on What's OK for You

Is there such a thing as neutral—something that neither uplifts nor tears down? I don't think so. Because people have different strengths, passions, personalities, and weaknesses, something that may not tempt one person could easily tempt another. For example, watching a football game is exciting and fun when your favorite team is playing. Or maybe you just enjoy sports. So, for you, watching a Sunday afternoon game recharges your battery. But maybe others become so caught up in the game they become angry when their team is losing. Their ranting goes on for hours after the game is over, and they take their anger at the team out on everyone around them. Not very entertaining or refreshing for anyone involved.

Another example is enjoying a meal out at a buffet. Some people have no problem a balanced meal of normal portions and enjoying a nice evening out with friends or family. Others lose the battle with temptation to gluttony as soon as they walk in the door of an all-you-can-eat buffet. For them, a restaurant where you can order from a menu might be a much better choice.

Overall, what we choose to let into our bodies, minds, and spirits affects us, one way or another. What starts out as "just one thing," "just one show," or "not too bad" can become habits that drain us. The enemy doesn't come at us with both barrels blazing. He lures us away inch by inch, step by step, choice by choice. Unless we're standing still—and that, to me, is a definition of lukewarm (Revelation 3:16)—we are either stepping *toward* God or *away* from Him. If we're not stepping toward God, we're not growing in His love. If we're not growing in His love, we can't protect ourselves and our relationships from the enemy's fiery darts.

Remembering God's Goal When Temptation Comes

Remember that the enemy's goal is to lure us away from God, one small seemingly innocent step at a time. He's not out to change us overnight—he reasons with us like he did with Eve in the garden—"Did God really say…"—so that we rationalize the compromise in our lives. He tempts us with what doesn't seem *that* bad and with what we've always done before with no problem.

Yet when we sin in some of these "small ways" we may be causing others to sin as well (1 Corinthians 8:9).

And remember, God is right there beside you and me, gently speaking to us about giving up or changing the entertainment choices we once thought were okay. When He does, obey Him. Obedience is the only way to continue to grow closer to the Lord and to stop the enemy dead in his tracks. I used to watch TV shows I thought were funny, but as I grew closer to the Lord I became uncomfortable watching them. The same thing was true for books I read and movies I watched. I won't name any here because they are my personal convictions, between God and myself. My goal is not to get you to adopt the same convictions, but to encourage you to seek God if you start to feel uncomfortable about what you watch, read, or listen to, and then obey what He tells you to do. I can't fully explain the spiritual dynamic, but I can testify from my experience. When I obey God and give up what He asks me to, I gain far more peace with God and an increasing ability to hear His voice than I lost in what I gave up.

A Gradual Decline

One of the best examples I can share about how the enemy slowly works in our culture to lure us away from God, is how movies have changed over the past 50 years or so.

Years ago, I had a vision related to the decline of morality in our country. I saw a sea of Rip Van Winkles rise up from cots, beards and all. Groggy, they rubbed their eyes, stretched, and started to get out of bed. As

I prayed for meaning, the Lord said, *My church doesn't realize how far this country has strayed from Me and from My ways. They need to WAKE UP.*"

My heart broke in repentance for the threads of compromise in my own life, in our culture, and especially in the church. I realized it happened in a gradual and masterful way so as not to arouse opposition. And we fell for it.

The next day, the Lord compelled me to research headlines and movies from the 1980s and compare them to the current day. What I found made perfect sense, and I could see how the enemy has used the media, over time, to lure us into complacency.

Before the 1960s, movies were governed by the Hays Code (see article in Wikipedia for details, https://en.wikipedia.org/wiki/Hays_Code). The code contained guidelines about making movies that would lift a society up, and *not* making movies that could lower moral standards. Movie producers recognized their responsibility to the public, and they recognized the power of movies to affect their audience. Isn't it refreshing to watch movies made in the 1930s through 1950s and know you don't have to worry about what you might see?

In 1968, Jack Valenti, then president of the Motion Picture Association of America (MPAA), responded to this "new era in films" by abolishing the "censorship" of the Hays Code and initiating the current rating system in the name of keeping with the times and being progressive. The result of the changes and unrest in the turbulent '60s was the emergency of a "new kind" of

American movie—blunt and open and made by film-makers subject only to self-imposed restraints.

The enemy didn't waste any time with the inch he was given. Movie makers pounced on their new freedom, and the enemy used them to keep methodically pushing the limits of acceptability. Instead of something fixed and stable, the "standard" for decency became whatever people were willing to accept.

One step at a time, over many years, what once was absolutely shocking became "not too bad." Our culture became desensitized to violence, sex, and foul language; and we excused scenes of totally objectionable content so we could watch a "good" movie. Instead of quality (does this movie have objectionable content?), we judged based on quantity (how many "bad" scenes or curse words are in the movie?) We tend to allow our children to see what we ourselves find objectionable, as long as it's not *too* much obscenity, nudity, or foul language.

Not So Gradual Decline

Fast forward to today. Once the shocking became acceptable in movies, it slid its way into our living rooms through our TVs…first only after 10 p.m., and now just about any time with cable and satellite TV.

Then the internet exploded onto the scene almost totally uncensored. Video games—violent, image-laden video games—became readily available. Today in our culture it is considered totally acceptable to curse, have sex with anyone who is willing (regardless of one's gender or sexual identity), be disrespectful and rebellious, and show all types of violence in the name of realism.

And now we have social media: Facebook, Twitter, Instagram, Pinterest, TikTok, and more. Social media can be a blessing used to spread God's truth and encouragement, and in keeping us informed and connected across the miles. We can enjoy pictures, be inspired, share recipes and family happenings. But it can also suck up our time, drive us to compete and stress over likes, and give us a false sense of connection and relationship with others.

With movies, TV, internet, and social media, we've come a long way, baby...and it's not always a good thing.

Choosing Wisely in All Areas of Entertainment

What we watch is not the only source of temptation; we must also wisely choose what we listen to, including music and news. Music is extremely powerful and it embeds itself deeply into our souls, especially songs we hear repeatedly. How many times have you heard a favorite song from the old days that you hadn't heard for ages and been able to sing along word for word, beat for beat? Do you think about the words you're singing? It's very tempting to listen to music because we like the beat. We also have to wisely choose news, podcasts, and other audio messages we take in because they are feeding our souls. Remember chapter 6 on the power of words? The words that leave our mouths, and the words we take in, are very powerful.

Years ago, early in my faith walk, I was driving through town with my windows down, listening to an '80s rock song. This particular song didn't have the "purest" of lyrics, and here I was singing at the top of my lungs. Mid-sentence, I stopped short. *What am I singing?* *Oops, probably not a good idea to listen to this.* Shortly after that, the Lord confirmed what I thought by asking me to completely stop listening to secular music and listen only to Christian music for a season. I had to be re-programmed. He wanted me praising Him when I first woke up, not singing about illicit love.

A few years later, He asked me to stop watching TV for a season. I called it mindless TV and watched it to relax, but He called it life-draining. He knew that it was filling me with images and words that took up valuable room in my mind and in my spirit. He had started giving me visions, and I couldn't see them clearly with so much clutter from TV and movies. Even today, I can tell if I'm taking in things I shouldn't by how I start to feel: apathetic, irritable, and lazy. Yes, I sometimes relax by watching TV or a movie, but I need to be careful of the content or I can easily fall into laziness.

How do you know when what you watch or listen to is becoming a problem? Examine your moods, thoughts, and behavior. Are you growing in the fruits of the spirit (Galatians 5:22-23), and enjoying healthy, God-centered relationships? Or are you increasingly frustrated and short-tempered, and feeling addictively drawn to songs, podcasts, TV and movies that you know deep down inside contradict the values you hold?

You CAN Overcome Temptation

God knows we'll be tempted, and He is right here with us. We can do as Jesus did and pray as he instructed us in Matthew 6:13: "And lead us not into temptation, but deliver us from the evil one." And we can ask for the way out as Paul spoke about in 1 Corinthians 10:13 (AMPC):

> For no temptation (no trial regarded as enticing to sin), [no matter how it comes or where it leads] has overtaken you and laid hold on you that is not common to man [that is, no temptation or trial has come to you that is beyond human resistance and that is not adjusted and adapted and belonging to human experience, and such as man can bear]. But God is faithful [to His Word and to His compassionate nature], and He [can be trusted] not to let you be tempted and tried and assayed beyond your ability and strength of resistance and power to endure, but with the temptation He will [always] also provide the way out (the means of escape to a landing place), that you may be capable and strong and powerful to bear up under it patiently.

God will answer our prayers for help by providing us with guidance and strength to overcome. Sometimes He'll miraculously intervene to rescue us from a tempting situation. But most of the time, we first must choose. He won't do for us what He enables us to do for ourselves. If we don't act on what we know to be true and turn from temptation, we are on our own.

Even a Little Can Be Too Much

I'll close with a sort synopsis of a story that has been circulating the internet for years. The original version of the story by the author can be found here: https://www.davidservant.com/brownie-surprise/

Two teenage boys asked their father if they could see a popular PG-13 rated movie. The father said no because the movie contained a few sexual scenes that are against what God values. The boys argued with their father that the scenes were short and hardly anything, but to no avail. That night their father offered them some home-made brownies. Right before the boys bit into one, the father said, "Before you eat, I need to tell you I put a small teaspoon of dog poop in the brownies. Hardly anything, you shouldn't even taste it."

Point made. Point accepted.

With God, There Is Always Hope

God is not surprised by our culture's continued decline. I believe He is saddened by the worldliness of His Bride, the Church, and our lack of response to the decline. His heart breaks over the lost who are confused, led astray, or rejected by His Bride's ungodly choices and culture.

But He is pleased by those who are willing to obey Him and willing to live before Him with righteous and pure lives. While the devil roams around like a roaring lion seeking people to devour (1 Peter 5:8), God calls us to make His disciples:

> Then Jesus came to them and said, "All authority in heaven and on earth has been given to me. Therefore go and make disciples of all nations, baptizing them in the name of the Father and of the Son and of the Holy Spirit, and teaching them to obey everything I have commanded you. And surely I am with you always, to the very end of the age."
> —Matthew 28:18-20

How can you and I make disciples of others if we are not living, ourselves, as disciples of Jesus?

Next time you want to relax and recharge, stop to think. Ask yourself this question: *Am I refreshing my soul or am I opening myself up to temptation?* Pray and ask God for His opinion. Then if you don't have peace about it, don't do it.

When you reflect back to a point in your life from months or years ago, you want to be able to say, "Wow—how did I get here from there?" and mean it in a good way.

The enemy is waiting and watching, seeking to devour all who will let him, one bite at a time. Resist Him by obeying Jesus. Consider these words from James 4:

> You adulterous people, don't you know that friendship with the world means enmity against God? Therefore, anyone who chooses

to be a friend of the world becomes an enemy of God. Or do you think Scripture says without reason that he jealously longs for the spirit he has caused to dwell in us? But he gives us more grace. That is why Scripture says:

"God opposes the proud but shows favor to the humble."

Submit yourselves, then, to God. Resist the devil, and he will flee from you. Come near to God and he will come near to you. Wash your hands, you sinners, and purify your hearts, you double-minded. Grieve, mourn and wail. Change your laughter to mourning and your joy to gloom. Humble yourselves before the Lord, and he will lift you up.

—James 4:4-10

It's never too late to make changes. Resolve to start today.

Dear Jesus,

Please let me know if I need to make any changes in my life with regard to music, TV, movies, news, or books I read. Help me to make the unpopular decisions for myself and my family on what we allow into our lives and our home. Teach me how to discern Your voice, and to follow it confidently. I want to be full of You and Your love, not the world and fear.

In Your name I pray, Amen.

9

Why We Fight

I hope the Lord has spoken to you as you have been reading. He has definitely spoken to me as I have been writing, and pointed out so many ways I've let the enemy into my closest relationships. Especially my marriage.

Sometimes I'd think that I was above being tempted by the enemy in a certain way. I knew better, after all. I know what I write to be true, and I believe every word. And yet, well, I'd let my guard down and fall. I'd make plans without consulting the Lord. I'd rush into ministry or projects, or even relationships, and find no grace there because God did not call me.

Again. And again. And again. Like we all do at times.

It doesn't matter how long you or I have known the Lord, how close we feel to Him, or what we're doing *for* Him. Anyone can be deceived into letting the enemy into their lives and relationships at any time if they don't seek the Lord in *everything*. Given that, I'd like to leave you with a few closing thoughts to ponder.

- Unmasking and defeating our common enemy is not a once-and-for-all thing. As long as we're on this earth, we're on the battlefield and in the fight. Every day.

- Reading God's Word to know God—not just to know facts—is essential to growing closer to God.

- As you grow closer to God, two things happen: 1) the enemy picks up his attack against you and your loved ones; and 2) you walk in more authority and power to defeat him.

- Obedience is key. God is the Commander-in-Chief, and He always knows best. Period.

- Faith grows as we obey; our willingness to obey grows the more faith we have. To the degree we choose to obey, God will grow our faith.

- What you believe will influence your actions. If you believe you have victory in Christ, you will. If you believe you can't change, you won't.

- What you believe changes as you grow closer to God by reading the Bible, praying, and obeying. How you respond to those changes determines when and how much you'll continue to grow... if at all.

No matter where you are in your spiritual journey, God is there with you. He will never leave you nor forsake you (Hebrews 13:5). He loves all of us with a fierce, passionate love that is above and beyond anything we can comprehend. God is love.

When we fight *for* those we love instead of against them, we win the little battles and enjoy relationships the way God intended them to be. We love like He loves.

With that in mind, let's go back to 1 Corinthians 13 and reword verses 4-8 by replacing the word *love* with God.

> God is patient, God is kind.
>
> He does not envy, He does not boast, He is not proud.
>
> He does not dishonor others, He is not self-seeking, He is not easily angered, He keeps no record of wrongs.
>
> God does not delight in evil but rejoices with the truth.
>
> He always protects, always trusts, always hopes, always perseveres. God never fails.

God is love, and we are His. One of my favorite Bible passages about God's great love for us is Romans 8:28-39 in the Amplified Classic translation. With this Love on our side, we can endure whatever comes our way.

> We are assured and know that [God being a partner in their labor] all things work together and are [fitting into a plan] for good to and for those who love God and are called according to [His] design and purpose.
>
> For those whom He foreknew [of whom He was aware and loved beforehand], He also destined from the beginning [foreordaining them] to be molded into the image of His Son

[and share inwardly His likeness], that He might become the firstborn among many brethren.

And those whom He thus foreordained, He also called; and those whom He called, He also justified (acquitted, made righteous, putting them into right standing with Himself). And those whom He justified, He also glorified [raising them to a heavenly dignity and condition or state of being].

What then shall we say to [all] this? If God is for us, who [can be] against us? [Who can be our foe, if God is on our side?]

He who did not withhold or spare [even] His own Son but gave Him up for us all, will He not also with Him freely and graciously give us all [other] things?

Who shall bring any charge against God's elect [when it is] God Who justifies [that is, Who puts us in right relation to Himself? Who shall come forward and accuse or impeach those whom God has chosen? Will God, Who acquits us?]

Who is there to condemn [us]? Will Christ Jesus (the Messiah), Who died, or rather Who was raised from the dead, Who is at the right hand of God actually pleading as He intercedes for us?

Who shall ever separate us from Christ's love? Shall suffering and affliction and tribulation? Or calamity and distress? Or persecution or hunger or destitution or peril or sword?

Even as it is written, For Thy sake we are put to death all the day long; we are regarded and counted as sheep for the slaughter.

Yet amid all these things we are more than conquerors and gain a surpassing victory through Him Who loved us.

For I am persuaded beyond doubt (am sure) that neither death nor life, nor angels nor principalities, nor things impending and threatening nor things to come, nor powers,
Nor height nor depth, nor anything else in all creation will be able to separate us from the love of God which is in Christ Jesus our Lord.

— Romans 8:28-39

I have one final thought for you, one that is the most important factor in your ability to live victoriously. Is Jesus Lord of your life? Have you given your life to Him and received salvation? Are you walking securely in a relationship with Him as His disciple? If you're not sure, read the following verses from Romans, then pray with a trusted friend to ask Jesus to take over the reins of your life.

For Moses writes that the law's way of making a person right with God requires obedience to all of its commands. But faith's way of getting right with God says, "Don't say in your heart, 'Who will go up to heaven?' (to bring Christ down to earth). And don't say, 'Who will go down to the place of the dead?' (to bring Christ back to life again)." In fact, it says,

"The message is very close at hand;
it is on your lips and in your heart."

And that message is the very message about faith that we preach: If you openly declare that Jesus is Lord and believe in your heart that God raised him from the dead, you will be saved. For it is by believing in your heart that you are made right with God, and it is by openly declaring your faith that you are saved.

—Romans 10:5-10 NLT

Let's end where we started, with this passage from 1 Peter 5, continuing on from verse 5:

All of you, clothe yourselves with humility toward one another, because,

"God opposes the proud but shows favor to the humble."

Humble yourselves, therefore, under God's mighty hand, that he may lift you up in due time. Cast all your anxiety on him because he cares for you.

Be alert and of sober mind. Your enemy the devil prowls around like a roaring lion looking for someone to devour. Resist him, standing firm in the faith, because you know that the family of believers throughout the world is undergoing the same kind of sufferings.

And the God of all grace, who called you to his eternal glory in Christ, after you have suffered a little while, will himself restore you and make you strong, firm and steadfast. To him be the power for ever and ever. Amen.

—1 Peter 5:5-11

In Christ, you have the victory. Go forth and conquer!

Acknowledgments

Thank you to my Mom and Dad, family, and friends for loving me just as I am, and living out the truth to me and to each other that our value is not in what we do, but in who we're created to be. I am blessed beyond measure by your love.

Thank you, Don, for your consistent and unconditional love, and for releasing and encouraging me to follow my dreams…even when it means we spend less time together because I'm writing. Thank you also for teaching me so much about spiritual battles, directly and indirectly, as we live through the joys and challenges of married life.

Thank you to my amazing editor and fellow writer, Cindi, for all your time, wisdom, and encouragement. You understand me and what I'm trying to say, and you help me stay true to Scripture and to my own style. So thankful you are on this writing journey with me!

Most of all, thank You, Jesus, for revealing Your truth and love to me in big and small ways every day, and for working in and through me even when I kick and scream. Thank You for the gift of writing—may I always use it for Your glory.

Recommended Resources

These are a few of my favorite books on prayer, spiritual warfare, and other related topics. I am including my favorite fiction books as well. All are currently available on Amazon.com. Enjoy!

Nonfiction:

Bait of Satan, John Bevere. (Charisma House; Anniversary edition, 2014)

Battlefield of the Mind, Joyce Meyer (Warner Faith; Revised edition, 2002).

Beyond the Veil: Entering into Intimacy with God Through Prayer, Alice Smith (Chosen Books, 2010).

Delivering the Captives: Understanding the Strongman and How to Defeat Him, Alice Smith (Bethany House Publishers, 2006).

The Gift of Forgiveness, Charles Stanley (Thomas Nelson 2002).

Intercessory Prayer: How God Can Use Your Prayers to Move Heaven and Earth, Dutch Sheets (Bethany House Publishers, 1996).

Making Sense of Spiritual Warfare, Eddie Smith (Bethany House Publishers, 2008).

Victory Over the Darkness: Realize the Power of Your Identity in Christ, Neil T. Anderson (Bethany House Publishers, 2000).

Fiction:

On the Edge: A Novel of Spiritual Warfare, Parker Hudson (Edge Press, 2011).

Piercing the Darkness, Frank E. Peretti (Crossway Books, 1989). (NOTE: Read *This Present Darkness* by Peretti first, this is the sequel.)

The President, Parker Hudson (Edge Press, 2013).

The Screwtape Letters, C. S. Lewis (Harper One; Reprint edition 2015).

This Present Darkness, Frank E. Peretti (Crossway Books; Revised edition, 2003).

www.ingramcontent.com/pod-product-compliance
Lightning Source LLC
Chambersburg PA
CBHW071522120626
46550CB00006B/2316